CRACKLE GLASS

Identification & Value Guide

BOOK II

Stan & Arlene Weitman

COLLECTOR BOOKS

A Division of Schroeder Publishing Co., Inc.

The current values in this book should be used only as a guide. They are not intended to set prices, which vary from one section of the country to another. Auction prices as well as dealer prices vary greatly and are affected by condition as well as demand. Neither the Authors nor the Publisher assumes responsibility for any losses that might be incurred as a result of consulting this guide.

Searching For A Publisher?

We are always looking for knowledgeable people considered to be experts within their fields. If you feel that there is a real need for a book on your collectible subject and have a large comprehensive collection, contact Collector Books.

Cover Design: Beth Summers
Book Design: Sherry Kraus

Additional copies of this book may be ordered from:

COLLECTOR BOOKS
P.O. Box 3009
Paducah, KY 42002-3009

-or-

STAN & ARLENE WEITMAN
P.O. Box 1186
N. Massapequa, New York 11758

@ $19.95. Add $2.00 for postage and handling.

Contents

Acknowledgments

This book would not have been at all possible, if not for the help of our very special friends from West Virginia. Roy and Dee Elmer, of Vagabond House of Fine Collectibles, who gave us many of our leads; Virginia Pridemore, of the Blenko Glass Company, who answered our countless questions, and when unable to do so, always found someone who could; Chris Hatten, head librarian of the Huntington Museum, who took time out of his very busy schedule to photograph most of the beautiful catalogs in our book; Eason Eige, former curator of the Huntington Museum of Huntington, who gave us much valuable information; Richard Blenko, Jane McMahon, Richard Blenko, Sr., and Matt Carter of the Blenko Glass Company; Robert and Donald Hamon of Hamon Glass Company; Bill and Frank Fenton of Fenton Glass; Charles Gibson of Gibson Glass Company; and Arnold Russell of the Pilgrim Glass Company.

We would also like to thank the following special people: Virginia and Carmen Monteforte of Bayville Gardens & Antiques of Amityville, New York; Virginia Wright of the Corning Museum, Corning, New York; Bobby Rockwell of the Rockwell Museum, Corning, New York; Charles Gillinder of Gillinder Glass Company, Port Jervis, New York; Frank Thacker of the Williamsburg Glass Company, Virginia; Alec Abramov of AA Antiques, New York City; Ken Wilson, Murial Fennimore, Patricia Stone, Gloria Moncer, Chas West Wilson, Madge Greenblatt, Esq., Wally Davis, Dorothy Watkins, Phil Kleinberg, and Carol Costa.

Special thanks to Cheryl and Joel Knolmayer and Joan and Dennis Davis for sharing their crackle collections with us. Dennis, we really appreciate the beautiful pictures of your collection that you took for our book.

Last but not least, we would like to thank Otto Franek of the Franek Art Studio for spending so much of his valuable time with us, sharing his crackling techniques.

About the Authors

Arlene and Stan Weitman are avid collectors of crackle glass. They now have over 1,600 pieces in their crackle collection. They also collect antiques and other collectibles. One of their serious hobbies is photography. Most of the photographs in this book were done by them.

Arlene has a master of arts degree in education. She has been teaching elementary school in Valley Stream, New York, for the past twelve years.

Stan has been a court reporter for the State of New York, Workers' Compensation Board in Hempstead, Long Island, New York, for the past twenty-seven years. He is also a certified appraiser of antiques.

Stan & Arlene Weitman
P.O. Box 1186
N. Massapequa, New York, 11758
Fax (516) 797-3039
E-mail scrackle@htp.net

Introduction

Crackle glass is no longer an unknown. Since our first book came out, crackle glass has exploded onto the antique and collectible market. We are told it is difficult to find in some areas of the country, and the prices have skyrocketed, even higher than our book prices. Your never-ending questions — e-mail, faxes, telephone calls from all over the country, and our desire to learn more about our much-loved collectible, motivated us to delve deeper into the world of crackle, and write this book. We discovered additional processes of making crackle (please see Franek Art Studio's history), different companies who crackled in the late 1800s into the early 1900s including West Virginia companies that were not included in our first book. As in the first book, this book contains an identification and price guide. Since crackle is being made today, we have added a section which will help the collector distinguish the new crackle from the old crackle. In addition, we have included a section on overshot glass, as overshot and crackle are interrelated. We are very excited about our new-found information, and we are delighted to be able to share it with you in this book, our second book on crackle glass.

Dating and identifying the pieces was easier to do this time, as we were able to obtain copies of many of the old glass catalogs. We know you will enjoy seeing these catalogs in our book. Most were photographed by Chris Hatten, librarian of the Huntington Museum in West Virginia. Several of the black and white catalogs were photographed by us, courtesy of the Corning Museum, Corning, New York. Unfortunately, we weren't able to find these catalogs in color. We know that, although they are in black and white, you will learn much from studying the different shapes and designs characteristic of the various glassblowing companies.

As stated, the prices have skyrocketed.

In a shop in upstate New York, we found the identical Pilgrim creamer and sugar set, featured in our first book, plate number 339, on page 131, for $175.00. In our book, we have it valued at $50.00 – 75.00 for the set. When we questioned the proprietor as to why these pieces were so high in price, he answered us, "It's crackle glass. The hottest collectible around. Someone will buy it for this price." Needless to say, we were not the buyers for that set. Remember, only you, the buyer, can decide what you are willing to pay. Our book should be used only as a guide, as should any other price guide.

When pricing the pieces, we enlisted the aid of glassblowing experts from all over the country. With their assistance and knowledge, we were able to price the pieces, taking into account many different factors. The prices are retail prices for items that are in mint condition.

Age and rarity are two factors which considerably increase a piece's value. Several pieces are from the late 1800s, early 1900s. Some are displayed in different museums such as The Rockwell Museum in Corning, New York; The Brooklyn Museum in Brooklyn, New York; and the Milan Historical Museum in Ohio.

In addition, we have pieces from the same period which are also extremely rare, and almost impossible to find, thus demanding a high value. They have exquisite enamel work on them, depicting animal scenes. The detail work on each piece is a work of art, which would beguile not only crackle collectors, but also antique and art collectors.

As stated in our first book, factors such as color, labels on pieces, and stoppers intact on cruets and decanters increase the value of a piece.

We hope you find this book as informative as our first one. We thank you for your support and desire to learn more about crackle glass.

The Manufacturers of Crackle Glass

Even after extensive research, we were still unable to discover the exact origin of crackle glass. As far as we know, as stated in our first book, the sixteenth century Venetians claim credit for the crackling technique. In the late 1800s, early 1900s, this process was copied, and crackle became very popular in Europe. Some of the European companies who made crackle, during this period were Moser, Loetz, Harrach, Rousseu, Stevens & Williams, Skansen, Colony Glass, and Tuscany.

Some American companies making crackle at the same time were Steuben; Hobbs, Brockunier & Company; Imperial Glass Company; New England Glass Company; Boston Sandwich; Fry Glass Company; Reading; and the Durand Glass Factory.

The pieces made during this period were truly pieces of art. They are not only very difficult to come by, but are extremely expensive to purchase. While doing research for this book, we were fortunate to acquire, over the course of two years, a collection of rare and exquisite crackle pieces created by Moser, Steuben, Loetz, Stevens & Williams, New England Glass Company, and Reading.

Some additional companies who made crackle that were not mentioned in our first book are Moncer, Bonita Glass Company, Jamestown Glass House, Williamsburg Glass Company, Viking Glass Company, Empire Glass Company, Gillinder Brothers, and Fenton Glass Company. Gibson Glass Company and Franek Art Glass Studio are still making crackle today.

The History of Crackle Glass

MOSER

About six years ago, we were at an antique show and saw several crackle pieces with enamel scenes painted on them. We were told by the proprietor that the pieces were either Mount Washington or Moser. We didn't purchase them, as they were very costly. We regretted not acquiring those pieces years later. To our surprise, about a year ago, the antique dealer who was selling those pieces, had several other hand-painted crackled enameled pieces, which we readily purchased. We then began researching, sending pictures of our pieces to distinguished people in the field of glass. They all told us that these pieces are probably Moser, not Mount Washington Glass Company, as Mount Washington, although recognized for its superb enameled glass, never crackled glass. They believe, Moser crackled glass in the late 1800s. Ludwig Moser opened his glasshouse in Dvory in 1893. It was called "Karlsbader Glasindustrie Gesellshaft, Ludwig Moser und Sohne." Ludwig Moser won several medals as he exhibited his work internationally. Ludwig's firm was inspired by the Art Nouveau and Art Deco periods (1870–1924). In the early 1900s, Leo Moser, Ludwig's son, was the director of the firm. He began experimenting with colors early in the 1920s. Colors such as alexandrite, amber, helolite, turquoise, beryl, dark red, royalite, smoke topaz, and lemon yellow were the product of the inclusion of rare elements. The firm merged with the Meyr's Neffe firm in 1922, and was forced into bankruptcy in 1933 as a result of the Great Depression. It is interesting to note that the Moser works and name were one of the first to be restored by the Czech government. Moser will always hold a strong world posi-

PLATE: 1
HEIGHT: 3¼"
COLOR: Cranberry
STYLE: Candlestick Holder
COMPANY: Moser
DATE: 1880s
VALUE: $300.00 – 350.00
REMARKS: From the collection of
           Cheryl & Joel Knolmayer.

PLATE: 2
HEIGHT: 3¼"
COLOR: Cranberry
STYLE: Bowl
COMPANY: Moser
DATE: Late 1880s to turn of
           the century
VALUE: $325.00 – 375.00

PLATE: 3
HEIGHT: 3½"
COLOR: Topaz
STYLE: Vase
COMPANY: Moser
DATE: Early 1900s
VALUE: $275.00 – 300.00

PLATE: 4
HEIGHT: 3¾"
COLOR: Light Topaz
STYLE: Pitcher
HANDLE: Drop Over
COMPANY: Moser
DATE: Early 1900s
VALUE: $250.00 – 300.00

PLATE: 5
HEIGHT: 4"
COLOR: Topaz
STYLE: Three-footed Vase
COMPANY: Moser
DATE: Early 1900s
VALUE: $350.00 – 400.00

PLATE: 6
HEIGHT: 4"
COLOR: Sea Green
STYLE: Vase
COMPANY: Moser
DATE: Early 1880s
VALUE: $250.00 – 350.00
REMARKS: From the collection of
            Cheryl & Joel Knolmayer.

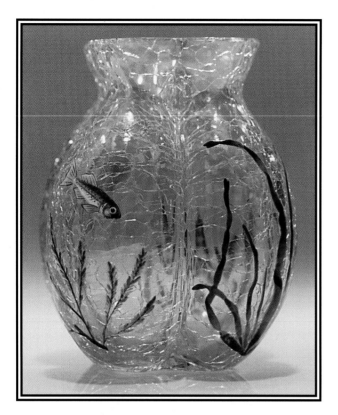

PLATE: 7
HEIGHT: 4¼"
COLOR: Topaz
STYLE: Vase
COMPANY: Moser
DATE: Early 1900s
VALUE: $300.00 – 325.00

PLATE: 8
HEIGHT: 5"
COLOR: Cranberry
STYLE: Vase
COMPANY: Moser
DATE: Early 1900s
VALUE: $375.00 – 425.00

PLATE: 9
HEIGHT: 5½"
COLOR: Iridescent Rose
STYLE: Candy Dish
COMPANY: Probably Moser
DATE: Early 1900s
VALUE: $250.00 – 350.00
REMARKS: From the collection of
             Cheryl & Joel Knolmayer.

PLATE 10A. Inset of Plate 10.

PLATE: 10
HEIGHT: 5½"
COLOR: Blue
STYLE: Pitcher
COMPANY: Moser
DATE: Early 1900s
VALUE: $550.00 – 650.00

PLATE: 11
HEIGHT: 6"
COLOR: Topaz Iridescent
STYLE: Pitcher
COMPANY: Moser
DATE: 1880s
VALUE: $450.00 – 550.00
REMARKS: From the collection of
            Cheryl & Joel Knolmayer.

PLATE 11A. Back of pitcher in Plate 11.

PLATE   12
HEIGHT: 5¾"
COLOR: Topaz
STYLE: Vase
COMPANY: Moser
DATE: Early 1900s
VALUE: $350.00 – 400.00

PLATE: 13
HEIGHT: 6"
COLOR: Light Topaz
STYLE: Vase
COMPANY: Moser
DATE: Early 1900s
VALUE: $275.00 – 325.00

PLATE 13A. Back of vase in Plate 13.

PLATE: 14
HEIGHT: 6½"
COLOR: Dark Blue
STYLE: Vase
COMPANY: Moser
DATE: Early 1900s
VALUE: $550.00 – 650.00

PLATE: 15
HEIGHT: 6¾"
COLOR: Topaz
STYLE: Pitcher
HANDLE: Drop Over
COMPANY: Moser
DATE: Early 1900s
VALUE: $350.00 – 400.00

PLATE 15A. Back of pitcher in Plate 15.

PLATE 15B. Inset of Plate 15A.

PLATE: 16
HEIGHT: 6"
COLOR: Cranberry
STYLE: Vase
COMPANY: Probably Moser
DATE: 1920s
VALUE: $350.00 – 450.00
REMARKS: From the collection of
Dennis & Joan Davis.

PLATE: 17
HEIGHT: 7½"
COLOR: Amber with Gold
Enamel Work
STYLE: Pitcher
HANDLE: Drop Over
COMPANY: Probably Moser
DATE: 1920 – 1940
VALUE: $150.00 – 200.00

PLATE: 18
HEIGHT: 13¼ x 7"
COLOR: Cranberry with White
& Blue Enamel Work
STYLE: Tray
HANDLE: Double Scallop
COMPANY: Moser
DATE: 1880s
VALUE: $1,000.00 +
REMARKS: Rare.

PLATE 18A. Inset of Plate 18.

PLATE: 19
HEIGHT: 10"
COLOR: Crystal with Enamel Work
STYLE: Pitcher
HANDLE: Reeded Drop Over
COMPANY: Moser
DATE: Early 1900s
VALUE: $600.00 – 800.00
REMARKS: Courtesy of Bay Village Gardens
           & Antiques, Amityville, Long Island.
NOTE: This is our favorite piece of Moser crackle.

PLATE 19A. Side of pitcher in Plate 19.

PLATE 19B. Inset of Plate 19.

LOETZ

In the late nineteenth century and twentieth century J. Loetz Witwe of Klostermule, Austria, produced iridescent art glass similar in appearance to the art glass of Louis Tiffany. Loetz was not only a contemporary of Tiffany, but prior to opening his own factory worked for Tiffany. Alexander Abramov of AA Antiques, New York City, who specializes in European art glass and porcelain, told us that Loetz crackled in the late 1800s. Not only is it extremely difficult to find Loetz crackle, it is also very expensive to obtain.

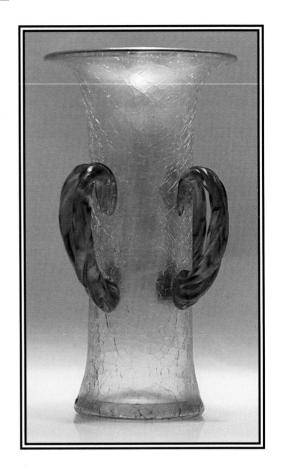

PLATE: 20
HEIGHT: 6"
COLOR: Crystal with Topaz Tinting
STYLE: Vase
HANDLE: (Four) Drop Over
COMPANY: Loetz
DATE: Early 1900s
VALUE: $1,500.00+

STEUBEN GLASS WORKS

On March 11, 1903, the Steuben Glass Works, named for the County of Steuben, New York, was conceived by T. G. Hawkes and Frederick Carder. In 1918, the firm was sold and was incorporated as a division of the Corning Glass Works. Carder served as its art director and designed many of the magnificent Steuben pieces that are displayed in the Rockwell Museum in Corning, New York. He was intimately involved in all aspects of glassmaking. Bobby Rockwell, curator of glass of the Rockwell Museum, stated that Steuben did not do much crackling. They began crackling glass in the mid-1920s and stopped in the 1930s. Crackling was done mainly as a side effect, and only as a special order. Steuben never crackled because of a defect (striation or cording in the glass), as they only used top-quality glass. In addition, many technical and artistic

innovations were used when crackling, resulting in different crackle styles.

One such style of crackle glass was Rose Quartz. This glass resembles the mineral for which it was named. The glass was usually heavy, about ¼" to ⅜" thick. Powdered glass gave the object its color. After it was crackled by a method of plunging the hot glass into cold water, it was then rolled into finely crushed rub frost and threads and reheated once more. The threads and frost were pulled into a textured effect with a hook and then it was marvered smooth. The mass was cased into a gather of crystal glass and formed into the final shape. There were additional processes added to this piece, but they did not have anything to do with the crackling of the glass. There is a beautiful piece of Steuben Rose Quartz in Paul Gardner's book, *"The Glass of Frederick Carder."*

Another style (Plate #21) can be found in the Rockwell Museum — the aventurine crackle vase. It is finely crackled, and has green with gold flakes and random bubbles throughout its body. It resembles the sixteenth and seventeenth century Venetian type of glass. It imitates the natural stone aventurine quartz, which sparkles and shimmers due to the flecks of mica or metallic particles embedded in to stone. In order to achieve the desired effect Carder mixed mica flecks into the aventurine glass. He achieved the crackling effect by dipping a gather of hot glass quickly into cold water, causing the glass to crackle in a random pattern. Bobby Rockwell, believes that this piece was a trial piece, as it was made according to Gardner's book about 1910–1917, before Steuben officially crackled glass. It is eight inches in height, and was probably a limited production item.

Also on display, in the Rockwell Museum, is the Steuben Aurene crackle. Aurene, which was made in gold, blue, brown, red and green will reveal thousands of minute fractures that both reflect and refract the light-giving iridescence when examined under a high-power glass. The matte finish is the result of tin and chloride sprays.

Still another Steuben crackle treasure exhibited in the Rockwell Museum is a Moss Agate vase. This style involved taking a gather of soda glass that was cased in lead glass to be coated in powder colored glass and again cased in lead glass. The piece was then injected with water which caused the weaker soda glass to crack. The water was then emptied out, and the piece was reheated leaving a network of cracks.

The amber and crystal vases with the green lion's heads attached are other examples of Steuben crackle. Steuben produced these vases in different shapes and sizes. Many companies in the early to mid-1900s copied the style vase. None, however, as far as we know, added the lions' heads to the sides.

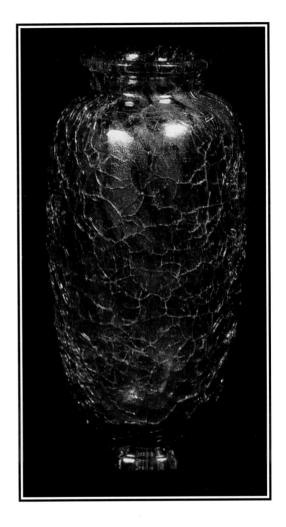

PLATE: 21
HEIGHT: 20 cm (8")
COLOR: Green
STYLE: Vase
COMPANY: Steuben
DATE: 1910 – 1917
VALUE: N/A
REMARKS: This is a green aventurine crackle vase, shape 2908 produced by United States, Corning, Steuben Glass, Frederick Carder.

We thank the Corning Museum for their contribution of this picture for our book.

PLATE: 22
HEIGHT: 5½"
COLOR: Crystal with Green
           Applied Lions
STYLE: Vase
COMPANY: Steuben
DATE: 1920s
VALUE: $750.00 – 950.00
REMARKS: From the collection
           of Dennis & Joan Davis.

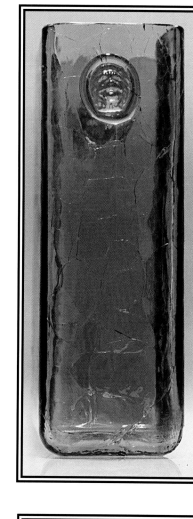

PLATE 23A.
Side view of
Plate 23.

PLATE: 23
HEIGHT: 9¼"
COLOR: Amber with Green Applied Lions
STYLE: Vase
COMPANY: Steuben
DATE: 1920s
VALUE: $750.00 – 950.00

PLATE 23B.
Inset of Plate 23A.

STEVENS & WILLIAMS

William Stevens and Samuel Cox Williams took over the Moor Lane Glass House in England in 1847, changing the name to Stevens & Williams. They moved the firm to Stourbridge in 1870, where they created a wide variety of artistic glasswares, crackle glass being one of them. In 1881, two great glass artisans, John Northwood, who tutored Frederick Carder, and Frederick Carder himself, worked at Stevens & Williams.

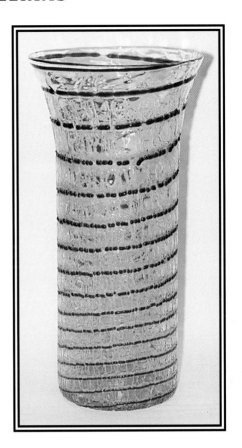

PLATE: 24
HEIGHT: 13"
COLOR: Crystal with Green Threaded Glass
STYLE: Vase
COMPANY: Stevens & Williams
DATE: 1880s
VALUE: $750.00 – 1,000.00
REMARKS: Courtesy of Alex Abramov of A.A. Antiques, N.Y.C. The green glass creates a pleasant contrast to the crystal crackle body.

DURAND ART GLASS COMPANY

Martin Bach of the Durand Art Glass Company, in the United States, claimed that in 1928, he manufactured Egyptian and Moorish Art Nouveau glass that were reproductions of crackle glass from those of ancient civilizations. They initially crackled lamp shades and globes for lighting fixtures. They soon started to reproduce vases and other decorative items, as the public responded so enthusiastically to this new type of art glass. Both the Egyptian and Moorish crackle were produced in a variety of colors and color combinations. The body glass was usually ambergris (waxy substance taken from whales). To make the Egyptian crackle, or Mutual crackle, the body glass was encased or threaded with heavy coils of opal, ruby, or blue glass. It was then placed

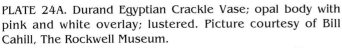
PLATE 24A. Durand Egyptian Crackle Vase; opal body with pink and white overlay; lustered. Picture courtesy of Bill Cahill, The Rockwell Museum.

on the blowpipe and plated over with different colored glass, and dipped into a vat of water. This procedure created the crackling of the outer layers of glass, forming fissures and cracks all over the gather. The glassblower reheated the gather and proceeded to blow it out, causing the cracks in the outer layers of glass to spread apart, and thus create the textured effect common to crackle glass wares. The glassblower then formed the object and sprayed it with a lustering compound. It is interesting to note that the Moorish crackle was made in a similar fashion, except it was not plated with opal glass.

FRY GLASS COMPANY

The H.C. Fry Company of Rochester, Pennsylvania, was in business from 1901 to 1934. Occasionally, the company was known to crackle items for enhancement.

The bodies of these items were usually white opalescent or crystal with cobalt, green, blue, black, amber, lavender, and pink additions, such as feet, knobs, spouts, and handles.

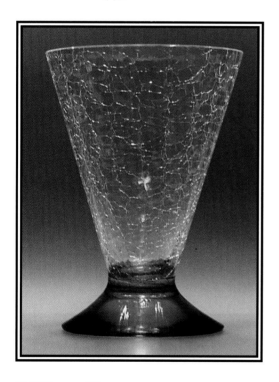

PLATE: 25
HEIGHT: 5"
COLOR: Crystal with Vaseline Base
STYLE: Glass
COMPANY: Fry
DATE: 1901 – 1934
VALUE: $50.00 – 75.00
REMARKS: Vaseline glass will fluoresce under black light. Vaseline glass increases the value of the piece.

PLATE: 26
HEIGHT: 5"
COLOR: Crystal with Cobalt Base
STYLE: Glass
COMPANY: Fry
DATE: 1901 – 1934
VALUE: $50.00 – 75.00

GILLINDER BROTHERS

Gillinder Brothers, Inc., to the best of Charles Gillinder's personal knowledge and old catalogs, crackled glass at least from the mid-1920s. The company was started in 1861 in Philadelphia and continues today in Port Jervis, New York. They are still currently manufacturing crackle glass — a light blue crackle vase for their gift-ware line. Items made previously included open-stock and private molds. They never had a catalog exclusively on crackle glass ware. They manufactured vases, lamp parts including bases and shades, balls, cylinders, both square and round, novelties, and table ware. In the 1940s and 1950s, he remembers that they crackled pinch glasses in two sizes. The common crackle colors included in their line were clear, amber, smoke, and various shades of green, blue, and red, or any color that was requested by a customer. Charles Gillinder told us, "One method of making crackle is a modification of the methods you described in the process section of your book *Crackle Glass Identification and Value Guide*. We currently limit crackle to items made in a paste mold. However, in the past, iron molds were also used. The glass is blown to shape, then before it is set up, removed from the mold, and plunged in the water. After it is removed from the water, the item is placed back into the mold to straighten and test for tightness. Crackle size is controlled in part by the water temperature. It should also be noted that in our experience crackle ware is made heavier than plain ware. This extra weight, from a practical standpoint, limits the size of crackle ware to equals of a 14" ball." We were told that they may stop crackling in the very near future. In the catalog section, you can see a picture of the light blue crackle vase still being made today.

PLATE: 27
HEIGHT: 8"
COLOR: Crystal
STYLE: Block Vase
COMPANY: Gillinder Brothers
DATE: Probably 1930s – 1950s
VALUE: $75.00 – 100.00
REMARKS: Courtesy of Gillinder Brothers.

WESTMORELAND GLASS COMPANY

The Westmoreland Glass Company was located in Grapeville, Pennsylvania. According to the Chas West Wilson's book, *"Westmoreland Glass Identification & Value Guide,"* Westmoreland crackled glass at least from late 1920 to late 1924. Some of the crackled items they offered were luster flower bowls, plates made in crystal and fancy colors, bowls in dark green, and beautiful baskets that were available in many different sizes. Crackle glass was superseded by mould crackle in 1924. Please refer to Chas West Wilson's book for a more in-depth history of the Westmoreland Glass Company.

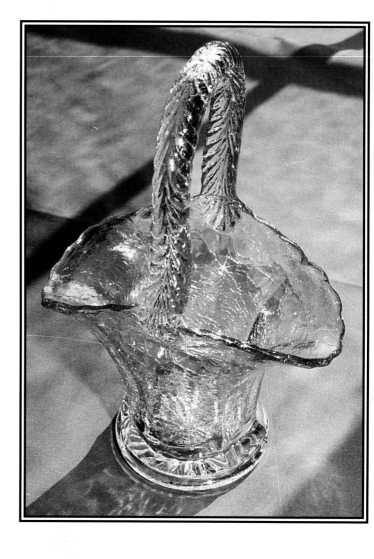

PLATE: 28
HEIGHT: 5"
COLOR: Crystal Lustre Stained
STYLE: Basket
HANDLE: Braided
COMPANY: Westmoreland
DATE: 1920 – 1924
VALUE: $85.00 – 110.00
REMARKS: Courtesy of Chas West Wilson.

PLATE: 29
ACROSS: 9½"
COLOR: Dark Green
STYLE: Bowl
COMPANY: Westmoreland
DATE: 1920 – 1924
VALUE: $60.00 – 85.00
REMARKS: Courtesy of Chas West
           Wilson.

MONCER GLASS COMPANY

Moncer Glass Company was a family owned and operated business. It was started by Ernest Oral Moncer, his two sons, Oral Edison and Franklin, and Oral Edison's wife, Gloria. Oral and Gloria Edison's children were also active participants in the Moncer Glass Company. In the Early 1940s the Moncer family built a plant in their backyard behind their Michigan Street, West Virginia, home. The plant remained operable until the late 1940s, when the family decided to close up shop and move to Florida. They came back to West Virginia in 1949, and again opened up a plant, this time behind their Washington Avenue house. They remained in business until the Early 1960s. When asked why they went out of business, Gloria Moncer stated, "The companies from overseas put us out of business." They crackled from the Early 1940s to the Early 1960s. Some of their crackled items were cruets, large pieces, decanters, "footed-lady dishes," and swordfish. Gloria Moncer told us that they made both free-blown and mould crackle.

BONITA GLASS COMPANY

Bonita Glass Company was located in Huntington, West Virginia, and was in operation from 1931 to 1953. Bonita crackled, as indicated in its catalog, glasses, vases, hats, and perfume bottles. Eason Eige, the senior curator of the Huntington Museum, stated, "Bonita pieces are often confused with those of the Rainbow Glass Company." We agree, as both companies were known for their ornate, but elegant and graceful pieces.

VIKING GLASS COMPANY

According to our Viking catalog, the Viking Glass Company was established in 1902 in New Martinsville, West Virginia. In 45 years, Viking grew from a tiny plant to a thriving business known for its handmade glassware (pressed and blown). Viking crackled glass from the 1940s to the mid-1970s, as did the Rainbow Art Glass Company, a division of Viking.

EMPIRE GLASS WORKS

Empire Glass Works was located in Ceredo, West Virginia. Please note that the Empire catalog is identical to a section of the Pilgrim catalog, as Empire was a subdivision of the Pilgrim Glass Company. It existed in the late 1950s to the mid-1960s.

IMPERIAL GLASS COMPANY

The Imperial Glass Company was organized in Bellaire, Ohio, in 1901. In the Early 1900s the Imperial Glass Company made carnival crackle glass. According to Bill Edwards, the author of *Carnival Glass, 4th Edition*, "Crackle was mass produced in great amounts, probably as a premium for promotional giveaways." Carnival crackle was made in a variety of shapes: bowls, covered candy jars, water sets, auto vases, punch sets, plates, spittoons, and a rare window ledge planter. Marigold is the most common color. Some of the shapes also came in green and amethyst. In our opinion, this form of crackle is very rare and thus highly collectible, as we have only found two pieces of carnival crackle in all our years of crackle collecting.

JAMESTOWM GLASS HOUSE

Frank Thacker, president and owner of the Williamsburg Glass Company of Virginia, was able to give us an extensive account of the Jamestown Glass House, located on Jamestown Island, Virginia, and the water crackle made at that historical site. He worked at Jamestown up until 1969, and then went to work with Robert Hamon of Hamon Glass in 1969. According to Frank, and the Jamestown brochure that he shared with us, in 1608, the Jamestown colonist set up a glasshouse as they felt glass would be an "industrial" venture. It was one of the first ventures by the English in the New World. In 1931 the surviving remnants of their original furnaces were discovered. In 1949, the area was thoroughly excavated, and in 1957, the Jamestown Glass House was established for the 350th centennial celebration of the original glasshouse. It was decided that the glasshouse should be located a few yards from the original remains, and that the glass produced there would closely resemble the type of glass manufactured in 1608. The plant was operated and put together by the glass companies, who donated labor, technical assistance, and supplies. Imperial Glass was the largest contributor, and Gerald Vann Dermark, from the Ericson Glass Company, became the supervisor. The glasshouse demonstration was only supposed to be in operation for two summers, the summers of 1957 and 1958, but it was so successful,

attracting tourists from all over, that it is still in operation today. In 1957 to 1958, a stamp seal stating Jamestown Glass House was embedded in the glass, applied when the glass was still hot. Paper labels were used after 1958 to the early to mid-1960s. In 1959, the National Park Service of the Department of Interior took over the plant. The income from the glassware sales were used for operation and maintenance of the exhibit. Frank stated, "Water crackle was their most popular item, but they decided to discontinue making it in 1968, as they felt it wasn't authentic for the 1608 period." It is extremely interesting to note that only four styles of glassware were crackled — the 5¼" jug, the 5¼" pitcher, the 5¼" pitcher vase, and the 5" vase. All of the glass made, crackled and standard effect, was green, and blown off hand without the use of molds. To obtain the color and texture of the 1608 glass a pre-mix material was used containing sand (600 pounds), soda (90 pounds), potash (90 pounds), litharge, lead (240 pounds), nitre (30 pounds), aluminum hydrate (9 pounds), potassium dichromate (11 ounces), and nickel oxide (2 ounces). Jamestown never had a catalog, but they did give out brochures like the one in our catalog and brochure section, enabling the tourists to order items by mail upon returning home from their visit to the factory.

WILLIAMSBURG GLASS COMPANY

The Williamsburg Glass Company is located in Williamsburg, Virginia, and owned by Frank Thacker. Frank told us, "Williamsburg Town was restored in the late 1930s by the Rockefellers to look like Williamsburg of the early 1700s. Everything from Jamestown was moved to Williamsburg in the 1700s." The Williamsburg Glass Company was created in 1969 by Kanawha and the Williamsburg Pottery, and Frank was the general manager. From 1969 to 1980 they blew

crackle consisting of pitchers, vases, sugar bowls and creamers, miniature pitchers, left-handed pitchers, fish, fruit, beer mugs, perfume bottles, and glasses. Occasionally, they would put an embedded seal on a piece, such as a pineapple, initials, or the Williamsburg seal. The Williamsburg colors are blue, light blue, cobalt, ruby, amberina, green, and amethyst. Frank bought the company in 1979. They started blowing crackle glass again in 1989, as people asked for it, but only in very small amounts. They do not and never did have a catalog. People visiting the glasshouse can see the glass being made, and can purchase pieces displayed in their gift shop. Many of Frank's pieces look like Robert Hamon's of Hamon Glass, as Robert Hamon trained Frank. Frank, however, told us he never used the sawdust method (as mentioned in our first book) in crackling glass. Below you will see a gift from Frank, a beautiful amethyst perfume bottle that he made for us.

PLATE:	30
HEIGHT:	4½"
COLOR:	Amethyst
STYLE:	Perfume Bottle
COMPANY:	Williamsburg
DATE:	1997
VALUE:	N/A

PLATE 30A. Insert of Plate 30.

PLATE 30B. Insert of Plate 30.

GIBSON GLASS COMPANY

Charles Gibson told us that he started his glassblowing career when he began working for the Bischoff Glass Company. He was just a kid out of school, and desired to learn the glass business. He then became a finisher for the Blenko Glass Company. In 1976, he opened up Gibson Glass, a small paperweight shop which only stayed in operation for a year. He reopened his business in 1982, and has been in business since. He has crackled and continues to crackle specific items such as bowls, fish, and cruets, never crackling the stoppers of the cruets. His pieces are not free blown, but blown into a mold, and always stamped GIBSON, and the year that they were made. Gibson crackle colors are red, cobalt, and green. There are only a couple of thousand pieces of Gibson crackle in existence, so any piece found is highly collectible and high valued. Gibson also made a limited amount of carnival crackle. Again, these pieces would be highly collectible due to their rarity.

PLATE: 31
HEIGHT: N/A
COLOR: Iridescent Cranberry
STYLE: Vase
COMPANY: Gibson Glass Company
DATE: 1990s
VALUE: N/A
REMARKS: Courtesy of Gibson Glass Company.

PLATE: 32
HEIGHT: N/A
COLOR: Blue
STYLE: Fish Vase
COMPANY: Gibson Glass Company
DATE: 1996
VALUE: N/A
REMARKS: Courtesy of Gibson Glass Company.

PLATE: 33
HEIGHT: N/A
COLOR: Blue Iridescent
STYLE: Cruet
HANDLE: Pulled Back
COMPANY: Gibson Glass Company
DATE: 1988
VALUE: N/A
REMARKS: Courtesy of Gibson Glass Company.

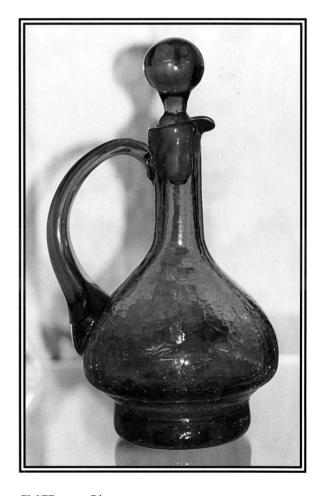

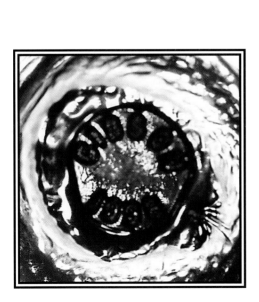

PLATE: 34
HEIGHT: N/A
COLOR: Blue
STYLE: Cruet
HANDLE: Pulled Back
COMPANY: Gibson Glass Company
DATE: 1990s
VALUE: N/A

PLATE: 35
STYLE: Stamp
COMPANY: Gibson Glass Company
DATE: 1988

FENTON GLASS COMPANY

The Fenton Glass Company has been around since the turn of the century. Operating first in 1906, in Martin's Ferry, Ohio, and then later in 1907 in Williamstown, West Virginia. The Fenton name is known throughout the glass-collecting world as it is one of the greatest glassblowing factories. They have designed and created a wide assortment of different types of glass from decorative to functional. They have produced over 130 patterns of carnival glass, custard, chocolate, opalescent, and stretch glass.

From 1992 to 1993, only for a year and a half, Fenton crackled glass. They crackled vases, urns, and baskets in vibrant pinks, blues, and greens. Each Fenton piece had a reflective quality giving it a gem-like appeal as an iridescent finish was applied after the glass was blown into the final forming mold. All pieces were stamped Fenton. They confirmed that they used the sawdust method for crackling. They also crackled some carnival glass.

When asked why Fenton Glass did not crackle back in the 30s, 40s, and 50s when everybody was crackling glass, Mr. Fenton responded that they did not choose to crackle glass as they wanted to do their own thing, not what everybody else was doing. We refer you to our catalog section to view the Fenton crackle pieces.

Fenton Art Glass Company is located at 700 Elizabeth Street, Williamstown, West Virginia. Telephone number (304) 375–6122.

FRANEK ART GLASS STUDIO

We recently had a very exciting experience that we would like to share with you. We were in Indigo Heirlooms Antiques admiring a beautiful amethyst miniature decanter. The proprietor, Carol Costa, recognized us as she purchased our book from us several months ago. She inquired if we were aware that a glassblower in the area was blowing new crackle glass. We contacted him immediately, and set up an interview date. While going to his studio, we were both excited and nervous. Excited because we knew we were going to learn more about our much-loved collectible, and nervous because we were afraid that the new crackle would look very much like the old, and even we wouldn't be able to tell the difference. We worried for naught. The crackle created by Otto Franek of Franek Art Glass Studio, is indeed, a work of art, but unique and different from the crackle made in the earlier years. Today, Otto blows crackle goblets, fish, and bowls.

Our interview began with Otto telling us that, "Crackle is a very, very big thing. There are so many different types of crackle. Timing is everything. If your timing is off, the crackling effect will be different." Otto

Franek was a Czech master glassblower. He came to the United States in 1969. "After the Russians came in, I went away." He has been in business at this particular studio (which, by the way, was a bakery before it became his studio) for one year. Previously, he worked in Riverhead, blowing glass animals. He does everything by himself; whereas, other studios have different people assigned to different glassblowing functions.

Otto told us that he knows of several different crackling methods. One method used by him is to blow the piece, and instead of dipping it into water, he rolls his pieces into wet sand. He then puts it back into the fire and goes back and blows it again into the mold, as the piece would bend out of shape. Rolling the glass in wet sand would produce very, very fine cracks. He also told us that the sand would scratch the glass a little bit, but you could not see the scratches with the naked eye. "This technique would produce a better crackle." Still, another method he uses involves the rolling of the glass into wet chips of wood. He told us the wood would make the crackle even finer than the process of rolling it in wet sand. The last process that Otto shared with us is the result of a crackle glass that we do not see often in our travels. This type of crackle is called peanut shell crackle. (The crackle looks like a Planter's Peanut shell, thereby giving it its name.) This effect is created by the glassblower crackling the glass before putting it into the mold. Please note the pictures below of Otto making us a Peanut Shell goblet.

PLATE 38. He is working the glass on a metal plate to smooth it out.

PLATE 36. Otto is getting a gather of hot glass onto the blowpipe.

PLATE 39. He is adjusting the glass on the blowpipe.

PLATE 37. He is blowing the glass.

PLATE 40. He is blowing the molten glass to make it larger, and he is further adjusting it on the blowpipe.

PLATE 41. He dips the molten glass into the water to crackle it.

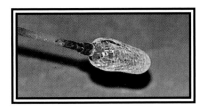

PLATE 42. This is the way it looks before it is put into the mold.

PLATE 43. Placing the glass into the mold, he now blows the glass to fill the entire mold.

PLATE 44. The glass entirely fills the mold.

PLATE 45. He is taking out the mold and checking it over to make sure it is symmetrical. (Notice the different tools in the background.)

PLATE 46. He is going back to the glory hole and taking hot molten glass and placing it onto the object. This is going to be the stem of the goblet. The temperature is between 1,800 and 2,200 degrees.

PLATE 47. He is working the stem and making the stem base.

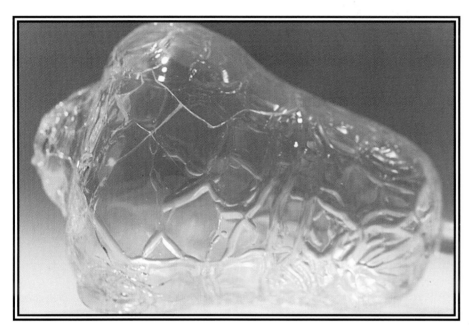

PLATE 48. This is the finished product.

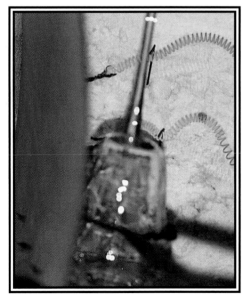

PLATE 49. The annealing oven where the piece is placed to cool down.

PLATE 50. Otto dipping the crackled piece into the colored powder.

Otto showed us some of the chemicals he uses, and some of the forms that they come in. For instance, to get the color cranberry, where other people today may use copper oxide because it is a lot cheaper, he

PLATE 51. This is the finished colored product.

still uses gold oxide. It comes in a rod, about a foot long, and about an inch and a half in diameter. He purchases these rods

from Germany, and pays about $55.00 for a kilo. In addition, he uses sheets of gold leaf, which are very, very fine sheets of gold paper that he places on certain pieces of glass. Otto confirmed what we always believed to be true that cranberry glass is the most expensive glass to make and buy. He told us that vaseline glass, using uranium oxide, is very difficult to get, and comes a close second, price wise, to cranberry glass.

Otto uses both glass made of lead and glass made of soda lime. If he wants finer cracks, he uses the soda lime glass. If he is designing a piece that requires a beautiful crystal-like shine, he uses lead glass.

The fish on this page was presented to us by Otto. On close examination, we stubbornly refused to believe that it was crackled. Instead of arguing with us, Otto made a similar piece, showing us that the fish is definitely crackled. The uncrackling effect, we found out, is created by the glassblower applying the coloring agent after the piece is crackled.

PLATE 52A. Inset of Plate 52.

PLATE: 52
LENGTH: 7"
COLOR: Orange
STYLE: Fish
COMPANY: Franek Art Glass Studio, U.S.A.
DATE: 1996
REMARKS: Courtesy of Otto Franek

If you would like to see Otto's beautiful creation for yourself, you may visit his studio at 61–18 Cooper Avenue, Glendale, New York, 11385, or you may call him at (718) 366–1183. He will be more than willing to share his expertise with you.

Vases

PLATE: 53
HEIGHT: 3½"
COLOR: Green
STYLE: Vase
COMPANY: Kanawha
DATE: 1957 – 1987
VALUE: $45.00 – 50.00

PLATE: 54
HEIGHT: 4"
COLOR: Cobalt Blue
STYLE: Vase
COMPANY: Unknown
DATE: 1940s – Unknown
VALUE: $45.00 – 55.00
REMARKS: Cobalt blue demands
           higher prices.

PLATE: 55
HEIGHT: 4½"
COLOR: Blue
STYLE: Vase
COMPANY: Probably European
DATE: Unknown
VALUE: $100.00 – 125.00
REMARKS: From the collection of
           Dennis & Joan Davis.

PLATE: 56
HEIGHT: 4¾"
COLOR: Amethyst
STYLE: Vase
COMPANY: Blenko
DATE: 1960s
VALUE: $60.00 – 85.00
REMARKS: Amethyst is a highly collectible
            color and warrants a higher price.

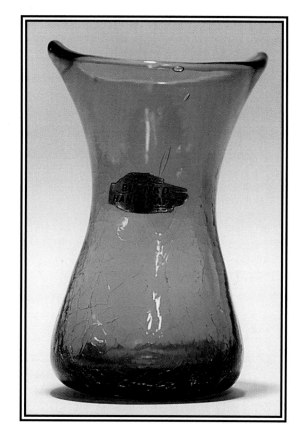

PLATE: 57
HEIGHT: 4¾"
COLOR: Emerald Green
STYLE: Vase
COMPANY: Blenko
DATE: 1960s
VALUE: $45.00 – 50.00
REMARKS: Labels increase the price.
            From the collection of Cheryl
            & Joel Knolmayer.

PLATE: 58
HEIGHT: 4¾"
COLOR: Smoke Gray
STYLE: Vase
COMPANY: Rainbow
DATE: 1940 – 1960s
VALUE: $60.00 – 75.00

PLATE: 59
HEIGHT: 5"
COLOR: Green
STYLE: Vase
COMPANY: Jamestown
DATE: 1959 – 1968
VALUE: $40.00 – 45.00
REMARKS: Labels increase the price.

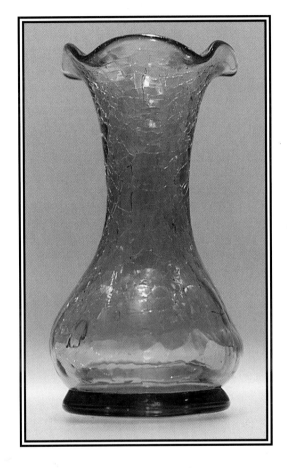

PLATE: 60
HEIGHT: 5"
COLOR: Blue
STYLE: Vase
COMPANY: Kanawha
DATE: 1957 – 1987
VALUE: $40.00 – 45.00

PLATE: 61
HEIGHT: 5"
COLOR: Crystal
STYLE: Vase
COMPANY: Bischoff
DATE: 1942 – 1963
VALUE: $50.00 – 75.00

PLATE: 62
HEIGHT: 5"
COLOR: Orange
STYLE: Vase
COMPANY: Rainbow
DATE: 1940s – 1960s
VALUE: $45.00 – 50.00

PLATE: 63
HEIGHT: 5"
COLOR: Tangerine/Amberina
STYLE: Vase
COMPANY: Blenko
DATE: 1950s
VALUE: $50.00 – 55.00
REMARKS: Applied leaves.

PLATE: 64
HEIGHT: 5"
COLOR: Blue
STYLE: Vase
COMPANY: Kanawha
DATE: 1957 – 1987
VALUE: $50.00 – 60.00

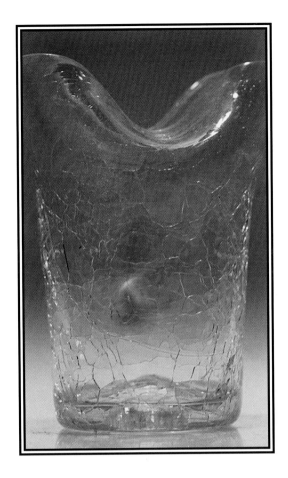

PLATE: 65
HEIGHT: 5¼"
COLOR: Crystal
STYLE: Vase
COMPANY: Probably Bischoff
DATE: 1942 – 1963
VALUE: $50.00 – 60.00

PLATE: 66
HEIGHT: 5¼"
COLOR: Cranberry
STYLE: Vase
COMPANY: Rainbow
DATE: 1940s – 1960s
VALUE: $65.00 – 80.00

PLATE: 67
HEIGHT: 5¼"
COLOR: Crystal with Sea
           Green Trim
STYLE: Vase
COMPANY: Blenko
DATE: 1950s
VALUE: $50.00 – 75.00

PLATE: 68
HEIGHT: 5¼"
COLOR: Yellow
STYLE: Vase
COMPANY: Kanawha
DATE: 1957 – 1987
VALUE: $45.00 – 50.00

PLATE: 69
HEIGHT: 5½"
COLOR: Blue
STYLE: Vase
COMPANY: Blenko
DATE: 1960s
VALUE: $50.00 – 60.00

PLATE: 70
HEIGHT: 5½" x 8¼" across
COLOR: Green Tint
STYLE: Vase
COMPANY: Probably Bischoff
DATE: 1942 – 1963
VALUE: $60.00 – 85.00

PLATE: 71
HEIGHT: 5½"
COLOR: Ruby
STYLE: Vase
COMPANY: Rainbow
DATE: 1940 – 1960s
VALUE: $55.00 – 75.00

PLATE: 72
HEIGHT: 6"
COLOR: Blue
STYLE: Vase
COMPANY: Bischoff
DATE: 1940 – 1964
VALUE: $50.00 – 60.00

PLATE: 73
HEIGHT: 5½"
COLOR: Blue
STYLE: Vase
COMPANY: Rainbow
DATE: 1940s – 1960s
VALUE: $50.00 – 65.00

PLATE: 74
HEIGHT: 6"
COLOR: Vaseline
STYLE: Bud Vase
COMPANY: Unknown
DATE: Unknown
VALUE: $50.00 – 75.00
REMARKS: Vaseline glass is highly collectible and warrants a higher price. Vaseline glass will fluoresce under black light.

PLATE 74A. Vaseline glass under black light.

PLATE: 75
HEIGHT: 6"
COLOR: Cobalt Satin
STYLE: Vase
COMPANY: Unknown
DATE: Unknown
VALUE: $85.00 – 110.00
REMARKS: From the collection of Dennis & Joan Davis.

PLATE: 76
HEIGHT: 6½"
COLOR: Blue Gray
STYLE: Penguin Vase
COMPANY: Possibly European
DATE: Unknown
VALUE: $100.00 – 125.00
REMARKS: Polished pontil.

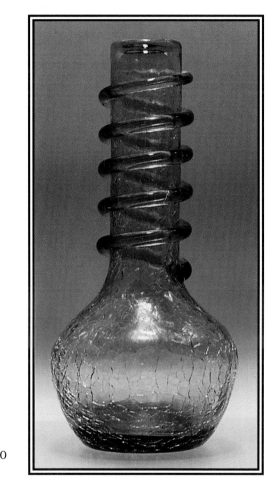

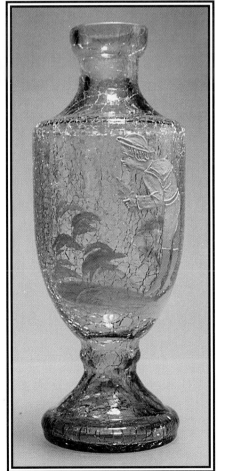

PLATE: 77
HEIGHT: 6¾"
COLOR: Olive Green
STYLE: Vase
COMPANY: Pilgrim
DATE: 1949 – 1969
VALUE: $50.00 – 75.00

PLATE: 78
HEIGHT: 7"
COLOR: Crystal
STYLE: Mary Gregory-type Vase
COMPANY: Unknown
DATE: 1880s
VALUE: $275.00 – 325.00
REMARKS: From the collection of Dennis
& Joan Davis.

PLATE: 79
HEIGHT: 7"
COLOR: Orange
STYLE: Footed Scalloped Vase
COMPANY: Blenko
DATE: 1940s – 1950s
VALUE: $120.00 – 145.00

PLATE: 80
HEIGHT: 6¾"
COLOR: Crystal with Green Tint
STYLE: Vase
COMPANY: Unknown
DATE: Unknown
VALUE: $110.00 – 125.00
REMARKS: Frilled top with white metal
              decorations — mold blown.

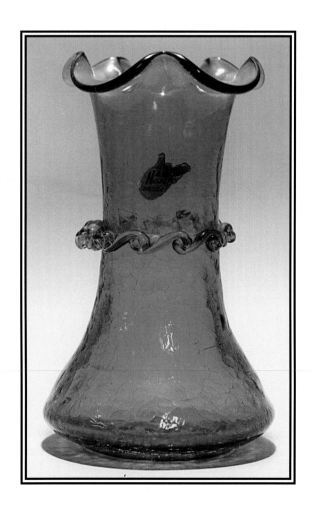

PLATE: 81
HEIGHT: 7"
COLOR: Emerald Green
STYLE: Vase
COMPANY: Hamon
DATE: 1940s – 1966
VALUE: $75.00 – 85.00
REMARKS: Labels increase the price. From the
              collection of Cheryl & Joel Knolmayer.

PLATE: 82
HEIGHT: 7"
COLOR: Crystal
STYLE: Double Handle Vase
HANDLE: Green
COMPANY: Blenko
DATE: 1960s
VALUE: $80.00 – 95.00
REMARKS: From the collection of
           Cheryl & Joel Knolmayer.

PLATE: 83
HEIGHT: 7¼"
COLOR: Amber
STYLE: Vase
COMPANY: Bischoff
DATE: 1950s
VALUE: $85.00 – 100.00
REMARKS: Note very odd top.

PLATE: 84
HEIGHT: 7¼"
COLOR: Emerald Green
STYLE: Vase
COMPANY: Pilgrim
DATE: 1949 – 1969
VALUE: $75.00 – 90.00

PLATE: 85
HEIGHT: 7½"
COLOR: Orange
STYLE: Vase
COMPANY: Pilgrim
DATE: 1949 – 1969
VALUE: $75.00 – 90.00

PLATE: 86
HEIGHT: 7½"
COLOR: Orange
STYLE: Vase
COMPANY: Rainbow
DATE: 1940s – 1960
VALUE: $60.00 – 85.00

PLATE: 87
HEIGHT: 7½"
COLOR: Amethyst
STYLE: Vase
COMPANY: Bischoff
DATE: 1940 – 1963
VALUE: $150.00 – 175.00

PLATE: 88
HEIGHT: 7½"
COLOR: Blue/Gray
STYLE: Vase
COMPANY: Blenko
DATE: 1958
VALUE: $80.00 – 90.00
REMARKS: Rare color.

PLATE: 89
HEIGHT: 7¾"
COLOR: Lemon & Lime
STYLE: Vase
COMPANY: Viking
DATE: 1944 – 1960
VALUE: $75.00 – 100.00
REMARKS: Labels increase the price. From the
            collection of Cheryl & Joel Knolmayer.

PLATE: 90
HEIGHT: 7¾"
COLOR: Tangerine/Amberina
STYLE: Vase
COMPANY: Blenko
DATE: 1950s
VALUE: $125.00 – 150.00

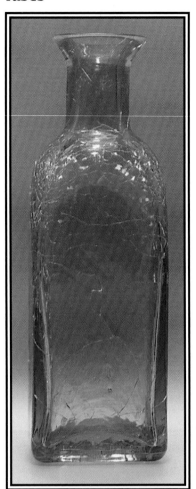

PLATE: 91
HEIGHT: 8"
COLOR: Blue
STYLE: Bottle
COMPANY: Unknown
DATE: Unknown
VALUE: $60.00 – 80.00

PLATE: 92
HEIGHT: 8"
COLOR: Tangerine/Amberina
STYLE: Vase
COMPANY: Blenko
DATE: 1950s
VALUE: $75.00 – 100.00

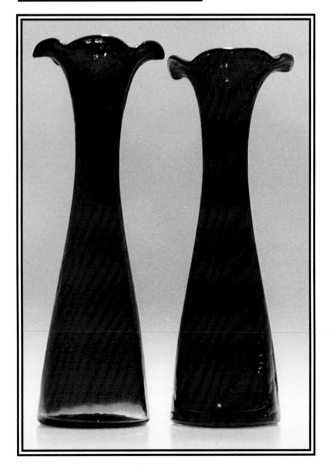

PLATE: 93
HEIGHT: 8"
COLOR: Amberina
STYLE: Vase
COMPANY: Kanawha
DATE: 1957 – 1987
VALUE: $75.00 – 85.00 each

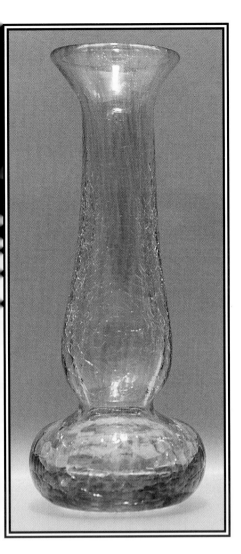

PLATE: 94
HEIGHT: 8"
COLOR: Light Blue
STYLE: Vase
COMPANY: Unknown
DATE: Unknown
VALUE: $75.00 – 85.00
REMARKS: Mold stamp on bottom (unknown).

PLATE 94A. Inset of Plate 94. We welcome coments on this mark.

PLATE 95A. Inset of Plate 95.

PLATE: 95
HEIGHT: 8"
COLOR: Crystal
STYLE: Vase
COMPANY: Unknown
DATE: Unknown
VALUE: $75.00 – 85.00
REMARKS: Made in Germany.
              Labels increase the price.

PLATE: 96
HEIGHT: 8½"
COLOR: Orange
STYLE: Vase
COMPANY: Blenko
DATE: 1940s – 1950s
VALUE: $120.00 – 145.00

PLATE: 97
HEIGHT: 8½"
COLOR: Blue
STYLE: Frilled-top Vase
COMPANY: Bischoff
DATE: 1940 – 1963
VALUE: $125.00 – 150.00

PLATE: 98
HEIGHT: 8¾"
COLOR: Crystal with Green Tint
STYLE: Vase
COMPANY: Unknown
DATE: Unknown
VALUE: $125.00 – 150.00
REMARKS: Frilled top with white metal
            decorations — mold blown.

PLATE: 99
HEIGHT: 9"
COLOR: Teal
STYLE: Vase (Fluted)
COMPANY: Rainbow
DATE: 1940s – 1960s
VALUE: $100.00 – 125.00

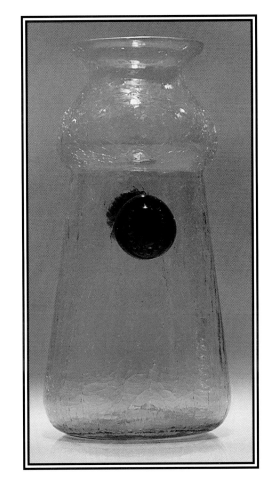

PLATE: 100
HEIGHT: 9"
COLOR: Chartreuse
STYLE: Vase
COMPANY: Probably Bischoff or Blenko
DATE: 1950s – 1960s
VALUE: $100.00 – 125.00

PLATE: 101
HEIGHT: 9"
COLOR: Crystal with Sea Green Base
STYLE: Flower Vase
COMPANY: Blenko
DATE: 1940s – 1950s
VALUE: $80.00 – 110.00

PLATE: 102
HEIGHT: 9¼"
COLOR: Lilac
STYLE: Vase
COMPANY: Blenko
DATE: 1940s – 1950s
VALUE: $100.00 – 125.00

PLATE: 103
HEIGHT: 9½"
COLOR: Crystal
STYLE: Vase
HANDLE: Red
COMPANY: Czechoslovakian Republic
DATE: Late 1800s
VALUE: $350.00 – 450.00
REMARKS: From the collection of
            Dennis & Joan Davis.

PLATE: 104
HEIGHT: 9½"
COLOR: Crystal with Green Snake
STYLE: Vase
COMPANY: Blenko
DATE: 1960s
VALUE: $100.00 – 125.00
REMARKS: From the collection of
            Cheryl & Joel Knolmayer.

PLATE: 105
HEIGHT: 9½"
COLOR: Dark Blue
STYLE: Vase
COMPANY: Blenko
DATE: 1960s
VALUE: $100.00 – 125.00
REMARKS: Scalloped top.

PLATE: 106
HEIGHT: 9½"
COLOR: Amethyst
STYLE: Vase
COMPANY: Hamon
DATE: 1940s – 1966
VALUE: $100.00 – 125.00
REMARKS: Amethyst is a highly collectible color
           and warrants a higher price.

PLATE: 107
HEIGHT: 9½"
COLOR: Crystal with Blue Leaves
STYLE: Leaf Beaker
COMPANY: Blenko
DATE: 1940s – 1950s
VALUE: $125.00 – 150.00

PLATE: 108
HEIGHT: 10"
COLOR: Crystal with Enamel Work
STYLE: Vase
COMPANY: Bohemian
DATE: Early 1900s
VALUE: $200.00 – 250.00
REMARKS: From the collection of
           Cheryl & Joel Knolmayer.

PLATE: 109
HEIGHT: 10"
COLOR: Sea Green
STYLE: Vase
COMPANY: Colony/Czechoslovakian
DATE: 1930s
VALUE: $100.00 – 125.00
REMARKS: Labels increase the price. From
           the collection of Dennis &
           Joan Davis.

PLATE: 110
HEIGHT: 10"
COLOR: Blue
STYLE: Vase
COMPANY: Blenko
DATE: 1940s – 1950s
VALUE: $80.00 – 110.00

PLATE: 111
HEIGHT: 10"
COLOR: Tangerine with Tangerine Leaves
STYLE: Leaf Beaker
COMPANY: Blenko
DATE: 1940s – 1950s
VALUE: $125.00 – 150.00

PLATE: 112
HEIGHT: 10"
COLOR: Crystal with Black Leaves
STYLE: Leaf Beaker
COMPANY: Blenko
DATE: 1940s – 1950s
VALUE: $125.00 – 150.00

PLATE: 113
HEIGHT: 10¼"
COLOR: Yellow with Orange Trim
STYLE: Vase
COMPANY: Blenko
DATE: 1960s
VALUE: $125.00 – 150.00
REMARKS: From the collection of
           Cheryl & Joel Knolmayer.

PLATE: 114
HEIGHT: 10½"
COLOR: Pink
STYLE: Vase
COMPANY: Unknown
DATE: Unknown
VALUE: $110.00 – 135.00
REMARKS: Rare color

PLATE: 115
HEIGHT: 11"
COLOR: Vaseline
STYLE: Vase
COMPANY: Unknown
DATE: Unknown
VALUE: $200.00 – 250.00
REMARKS: From the collection of
            Dennis & Joan Davis.

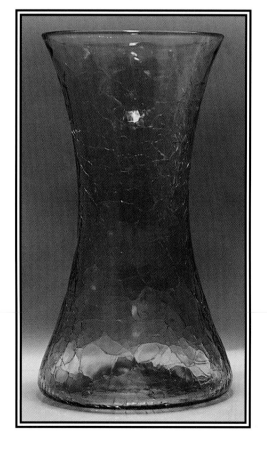

PLATE: 116
HEIGHT: 11"
COLOR: Rose Crystal
STYLE: Vase
COMPANY: Blenko
DATE: 1950s
VALUE: $110.00 – 135.00
REMARKS: Rare color.

PLATE: 117
HEIGHT: 11½"
COLOR: Amberina
STYLE: Bottle Vase
COMPANY: Blenko
DATE: 1960s
VALUE: $85.00 – 100.00

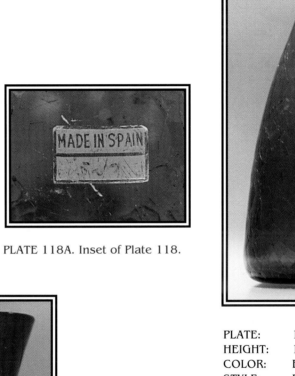

PLATE 118A. Inset of Plate 118.

PLATE: 118
HEIGHT: 11½"
COLOR: Emerald Green
STYLE: Bottle
COMPANY: Unknown
DATE: Unknown
VALUE: $85.00 – 100.00
REMARKS: Made in Spain. Polished
pontil. Labels increase
the price.

PLATE: 119
HEIGHT: 12¼"
COLOR: Tangerine
STYLE: Vase
COMPANY: Blenko
DATE: 1960s
VALUE: $110.00 – 125.00

55

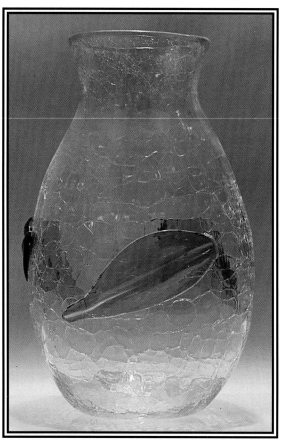

PLATE: 120
HEIGHT: 13"
COLOR: Crystal
STYLE: Leaf Beaker
COMPANY: Blenko
DATE: 1940s – 1950s
VALUE: $150.00 – 175.00

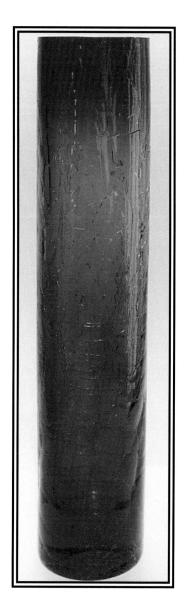

PLATE: 121
HEIGHT: 13"
COLOR: Amberina
STYLE: Vase
COMPANY: Unknown
DATE: Unknown
VALUE: $110.00 – 125.00
REMARKS: From the collection of Dennis & Joan Davis.

PLATE: 122
HEIGHT: 13"
COLOR: Green with Crystal Foot
STYLE: Vase
COMPANY: Probably European
DATE: Unknown
VALUE: $150.00 – 200.00

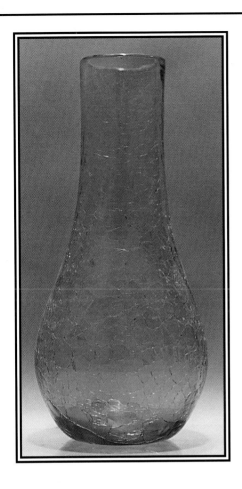

PLATE: 123
HEIGHT: 13½"
COLOR: Yellow
STYLE: Vase
COMPANY: Blenko
DATE: 1940s – 1950s
VALUE: $100.00 – 125.00

PLATE: 124
HEIGHT: 13½"
COLOR: Orange
STYLE: Footed Vase
COMPANY: Unknown
DATE: Unknown
VALUE: $175.00 – 200.00
REMARKS: Possibly European.

PLATE: 125
HEIGHT: 16¼"
COLOR: Smoke Gray
STYLE: Vase
COMPANY: Blenko
DATE: 1960s
VALUE: $150.00 – 175.00
REMARKS: Labels increase the
price. Rare color.

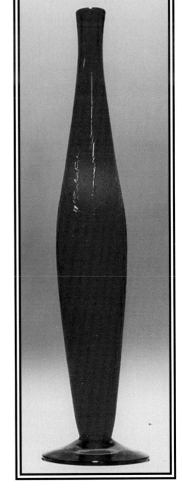

PLATE: 126
HEIGHT: 17"
COLOR: Tangerine
STYLE: Vase
COMPANY: Blenko
DATE: 1960s
VALUE: $150.00 – 175.00
REMARKS: From the collection
of Cheryl & Joel
Knolmayer.

57

PLATE: 127
HEIGHT: 3"
COLOR: Blue
STYLE: Creamer
HANDLE: Drop Over
COMPANY: Rainbow
DATE: 1957 – 1987
VALUE: $35.00 – 40.00

PLATE: 128
HEIGHT: 3"
COLOR: Emerald Green
STYLE: Creamer
HANDLE: Drop Over
COMPANY: Pilgrim
DATE: 1949 – 1969
VALUE: $35.00 – 40.00

PLATE: 129
HEIGHT: 3"
COLOR: Blue
STYLE: Miniature Pitcher
HANDLE: Drop Over
COMPANY: Probably Rainbow
DATE: 1940 – 1960s
VALUE: $35.00 – 40.00

PLATE: 130
HEIGHT: 3¼"
COLOR: Amberina
STYLE: Miniature Pitcher
HANDLE: Pulled Back
COMPANY: Kanawha
DATE: 1957 – 1987
VALUE: $40.00 – 45.00

PLATE: 131
HEIGHT: 3¼"
COLOR: Amberina
STYLE: Miniature Pitcher
HANDLE: Drop Over
COMPANY: Kanawha
DATE: 1957 – 1987
VALUE: $40.00 – 45.00

PLATE: 132
HEIGHT: 3½"
COLOR: Amberina
STYLE: Miniature Pitcher
HANDLE: Ribbed Drop Over
COMPANY: Pilgrim
DATE: 1949 – 1969
VALUE: $45.00 – 50.00
REMARKS: Ribbed handle pieces are priced higher.

PLATE: 133
HEIGHT: 3½"
COLOR: Orange
STYLE: Miniature Pitcher
HANDLE: Drop Over
COMPANY: Empire
DATE: 1970s
VALUE: $45.00 – 50.00
REMARKS: Empire was a division of the Pilgrim
Glass Company, and ceased doing business in the
1970s. Labels increase price.

PLATE: 134
HEIGHT: 3½"
COLOR: Amberina
STYLE: Miniature Pitcher
HANDLE: Ribbed Drop Over
COMPANY: Pilgrim
DATE: 1949 – 1969
VALUE: $45.00 – 50.00

PLATE: 135
HEIGHT: 3½"
COLOR: Amber
STYLE: Pitcher
HANDLE: Drop Over
COMPANY: Rainbow
DATE: 1957 – 1987
VALUE: $40.00 – 45.00

PLATE: 136
HEIGHT: 3½"
COLOR: Amberina (Satin Finish)
STYLE: Pitcher
HANDLE: Drop Over
COMPANY: Pilgrim
DATE: 1949 – 1969
VALUE: $50.00 – 60.00

PLATE: 137
HEIGHT: 3½"
COLOR: Topaz
STYLE: Miniature Pitcher
HANDLE: Drop Over
COMPANY: Pilgrim
DATE: 1949 – 1969
VALUE: $40.00 – 45.00
REMARKS: Frilled top and odd shaped handle.

PLATE: 138
HEIGHT: 3½"
COLOR: Sea Green
STYLE: Miniature Pitcher
HANDLE: Crystal Reverse Seven
COMPANY: Pilgrim
DATE: 1949 – 1969
VALUE: $40.00 – 45.00

PLATE: 139
HEIGHT: 3¾"
COLOR: Amberina
STYLE: Miniature Pitcher
HANDLE: Drop Over
COMPANY: Kanawha
DATE: 1957 – 1987
VALUE: $40.00 – 45.00

PLATE: 140
HEIGHT: 3¾"
COLOR: Amberina
STYLE: Miniature Pitcher
HANDLE: Drop Over
COMPANY: Rainbow
DATE: 1940s – 1960s
VALUE: $40.00 – 45.00

PLATE: 141
HEIGHT: 3¾"
COLOR: Topaz
STYLE: Miniature Pitcher
HANDLE: Crystal Drop Over
COMPANY: Unknown
DATE: Unknown
VALUE: $40.00 – 45.00

PLATE: 142
HEIGHT: 4"
COLOR: Vaseline Yellow
STYLE: Pitcher
HANDLE: Pulled Back
COMPANY: Rainbow
DATE: 1940s – 1960s
VALUE: $45.00 – 50.00
REMARKS: Unique color.

PLATE: 143
HEIGHT: 4¼"
COLOR: Satin Green
STYLE: Miniature Pitcher
HANDLE: Pulled Back
COMPANY: Kanawha
DATE: 1957 – 1987
VALUE: $50.00 – 60.00
REMARKS: From the collection of
            Cheryl & Joel Knolmayer.

PLATE: 144
HEIGHT: 4½"
COLOR: Cranberry
STYLE: Miniature Pitcher
HANDLE: Crystal Drop Over
COMPANY: Kanawha
DATE: 1957 – 1987
VALUE: $60.00 – 75.00
REMARKS: From the collection of
            Cheryl & Joel Knolmayer.
NOTE: Cranberry was made with gold.

PLATE: 145
HEIGHT: 4½"
COLOR: Satin Blue
STYLE: Miniature Pitcher
HANDLE: Pulled Back
COMPANY: Kanawha
DATE: 1957 – 1987
VALUE: $50.00 – 60.00
REMARKS: From the collection of
            Cheryl & Joel Knolmayer.

PLATE: 146
HEIGHT: 4½"
COLOR: Amberina
STYLE: Miniature Pitcher
HANDLE: Drop Over
COMPANY: Pilgrim
DATE: 1949 – 1969
VALUE: $45.00 – 50.00
REMARKS: Left-handed, rare. Note location of spout.

PLATE: 147
HEIGHT: 4½"
COLOR: Amethyst
STYLE: Miniature Pitcher
HANDLE: Drop Over
COMPANY: Pilgrim
DATE: 1949 – 1969
VALUE: $55.00 – 65.00
REMARKS: Amethyst warrants a higher price.

PLATE: 148
HEIGHT: 4½"
COLOR: Amethyst
STYLE: Miniature Pitcher
HANDLE: Drop Over
COMPANY: Rainbow
DATE: 1940 – 1960s
VALUE: $55.00 – 65.00
REMARKS: Amethyst warrants a higher price.

PLATE: 149
HEIGHT: 4½"
COLOR: Amberina
STYLE: Miniature Pitcher
HANDLE: Pulled Back
COMPANY: Hamon
DATE: 1940s – 1966
VALUE: $50.00 – 55.00
REMARKS: Note unusual coloration of amberina.

PLATE: 150
HEIGHT: 4½"
COLOR: Crystal
STYLE: Miniature Pitcher
HANDLE: Blue Drop Over
COMPANY: Kanawha
DATE: 1957 – 1987
VALUE: $45.00 – 50.00

PLATE: 151
HEIGHT: 4½"
COLOR: Blue
STYLE: Miniature Pitcher
HANDLE: Drop Over
COMPANY: Pilgrim
DATE: 1949 – 1969
VALUE: $45.00 – 50.00
REMARKS: Left-handed, rare.
Note location of spout.

PLATE: 152
HEIGHT: 4½"
COLOR: Multicolor
STYLE: Miniature Pitcher
HANDLE: Drop Over
COMPANY: Unknown
DATE: Unknown
VALUE: $75.00 – 100.00
REMARKS: From the collection of
Dennis & Joan Davis.

PLATE: 153
HEIGHT: 4¾"
COLOR: Sea Green
STYLE: Pitcher
HANDLE: Pulled Back
COMPANY: Stockholms Blasbruk (Skansen)
DATE: Unknown
VALUE: $55.00 – 75.00
REMARKS: Labels increase price. Polished pontil.

PLATE: 154
HEIGHT: 4¾"
COLOR: Amethyst
STYLE: Pitcher
HANDLE: Pulled Back
COMPANY: Rainbow
DATE: 1940s – 1960s
VALUE: $60.00 – 65.00
REMARKS: Amethyst is a highly collectible color and warrants a higher price.

PLATE: 155
HEIGHT: 4¾"
COLOR: Amberina
STYLE: Pitcher
HANDLE: Crystal Drop Over
COMPANY: Kanawha
DATE: 1957 – 1987
VALUE: $45.00 – 50.00

PLATE: 156
HEIGHT: 5"
COLOR: Butterscotch
STYLE: Pitcher
HANDLE: Crystal Drop Over
COMPANY: Heritage
VALUE: $50.00 – 60.00
REMARKS: Labels increase the price. From the collection of Cheryl & Joel Knolmayer.

PLATE: 157
HEIGHT: 5"
COLOR: Amberina
STYLE: Pitcher
HANDLE: Yellow Drop Over
COMPANY: Rainbow
DATE: 1940s – 1960
VALUE: $50.00 – 55.00

PLATE: 158
HEIGHT: 5"
COLOR: Green
STYLE: Pitcher
HANDLE: Pulled Back
COMPANY: Rainbow
DATE: 1940s – 1960s
VALUE: $45.00 – 50.00

PLATE: 159
HEIGHT: 5"
COLOR: Amberina
STYLE: Pitcher
HANDLE: Pulled Back
VALUE: $50.00 – 60.00
REMARKS: From the collection of
            Dennis & Joan Davis.

PLATE: 160
HEIGHT: 5"
COLOR: Cranberry with Yellow Swirls
STYLE: Pitcher
HANDLE: Drop Over
COMPANY: The Northwood Company
DATE: 1899 – 1923
VALUE: $100.00 – 150.00
REMARKS: Rare Find. From the collection of
            Dennis & Joan Davis.

PLATE: 161
HEIGHT: 5¼"
COLOR: Blue Green
STYLE: Pitcher
HANDLE: Drop Over
COMPANY: Rainbow
DATE: 1950s
VALUE: $45.00 – 50.00

PLATE: 162
HEIGHT: 5¼"
COLOR: Lemon Lime with Opalescent Top
STYLE: Pitcher
HANDLE: Crystal Drop Over
COMPANY: Pilgrim
DATE: 1949 – 1969
VALUE: $60.00 – 65.00

PLATE: 163
HEIGHT: 5¼"
COLOR: Amethyst
STYLE: Pitcher
COMPANY: Hamon
DATE: 1940s – 1966
VALUE: $65.00 – 70.00
REMARKS: Amethyst warrants a higher price.

PLATE: 164
HEIGHT: 5¼"
COLOR: Topaz
STYLE: Pitcher
HANDLE: Pulled Back
COMPANY: Viking
DATE: 1944 – 1960
VALUE: $50.00 – 55.00
REMARKS: From the collection of Cheryl & Joel Knolmayer.

PLATE: 165
HEIGHT: 5¼"
COLOR: Green
STYLE: Pitcher
HANDLE: Drop Over
COMPANY: Kanawha
DATE: 1957 – 1987
VALUE: $45.00 – 50.00

PLATE: 166
HEIGHT: 5¼"
COLOR: Crystal
STYLE: Pitcher
HANDLE: Amber Drop Over
COMPANY: Hamon
DATE: 1960s
VALUE: $45.00 – 50.00

PLATE: 167
HEIGHT: 5¼"
COLOR: Lemon Lime
STYLE: Pitcher
HANDLE: Pulled Back
COMPANY: Rainbow
DATE: 1940s – 1960s
VALUE: $60.00 – 80.00
REMARKS: Unusual color combination. Courtesy of Bayvillage
Gardens & Antiques, Amityville, Long Island.

PLATE: 168
HEIGHT: 5½"
COLOR: Cranberry
STYLE: Pitcher
HANDLE: Pulled Back
COMPANY: Kanawha
DATE: 1957 – 1987
VALUE: $75.00 – 100.00
REMARKS: "Authentic Cranberry Glass – The subtle color
            is produced with gold and then it is encased in
            pure crystal to add beauty to its delicate color"
            Kanawha Glass Catalog.

PLATE: 169
HEIGHT: 5½"
COLOR: Green
STYLE: Double Handled Pitcher
HANDLE: Drop Over
COMPANY: Jamestown
DATE: 1950s
VALUE: $55.00 – 60.00
REMARKS: From the collection of
            Cheryl & Joel Knolmayer.

PLATE: 170
HEIGHT: 5½"
COLOR: Blue
STYLE: Pitcher
HANDLE: Pulled Back
COMPANY: Hamon
DATE: 1960s
VALUE: $50.00 – 60.00

PLATE: 171
HEIGHT: 5½"
COLOR: Ruby
STYLE: Pitcher
HANDLE: Yellow Drop Over
COMPANY: Blenko
DATE: 1960s
VALUE: $50.00 – 60.00

PLATE: 172
HEIGHT: 5¾"
COLOR: Cobalt Blue
STYLE: Pitcher
HANDLE: Pulled Back
COMPANY: Hamon/Kanawha Catalog
DATE: 1940s – 1970s
VALUE: $75.00 – 85.00
REMARKS: Cobalt blue is rare and
            therefore warrants a higher price

PLATE: 173
HEIGHT: 5¾"
COLOR: Cobalt Blue
STYLE: Pitcher
HANDLE: Pulled Back
COMPANY: Hamon
DATE: 1940s – 1970s
VALUE: $75.00 – 85.00
REMARKS: Cobalt blue is rare and
            therefore warrants a higher price.

PLATE: 174
HEIGHT: 5¾"
COLOR: Tangerine
STYLE: Pitcher
HANDLE: Yellow Drop Over
COMPANY: Blenko
DATE: 1960s
VALUE: $55.00 – 65.00

PLATE 176A. Inset of Plate 176 – pontil.

PLATE: 175
HEIGHT: 6"
COLOR: Blue
STYLE: Pitcher
HANDLE: Drop Over
COMPANY: Greenwich
DATE: 1950s
VALUE: $60.00 – 65.00
REMARKS: Labels increase price. From the
collection of Cheryl & Joel Knolmayer.

PLATE: 176
HEIGHT: 6"
COLOR: Crystal
STYLE: Pitcher
HANDLE: Drop Over
COMPANY: Probably European
DATE: Unknown
VALUE: $60.00 – 65.00
REMARKS: Very large polished pontil.

PLATE: 177
HEIGHT: 6"
COLOR: Blue
STYLE: Pitcher
HANDLE: Crystal
COMPANY: Rainbow
DATE: 1940 – 1960s
VALUE: $65.00 – 70.00

PLATE: 178
HEIGHT: 6"
COLOR: Yellow
STYLE: Pitcher
HANDLE: Pulled Back
COMPANY: Kanawha
DATE: 1957 – 1987
VALUE: $60.00 – 65.00

PLATE: 179
HEIGHT: 6¼"
COLOR: Satin Lemon Drop Yellow
STYLE: Pitcher
HANDLE: Pulled Back
COMPANY: Kanawha
DATE: 1957 – 1987
VALUE: $65.00 – 75.00
REMARKS: From the collection of
           Cheryl & Joel Knolmayer.

PLATE: 180
HEIGHT: 6"
COLOR: Amberina
STYLE: Pitcher
HANDLE: Pulled Back
COMPANY: Rainbow
DATE: 1957 – 1987
VALUE: $60.00 – 65.00

PLATE: 181
HEIGHT: 6½"
COLOR: Amethyst
STYLE: Pitcher
HANDLE: Drop Over
COMPANY: Rainbow
DATE: 1940 – 1960s
VALUE: $70.00 – 80.00
REMARKS: Amethyst warrants a higher price.

PLATE: 182
HEIGHT: 6½"
COLOR: Satin Amberina
STYLE: Pitcher
HANDLE: Pulled Back
COMPANY: Kanawha
DATE: 1957 – 1987
VALUE: $65.00 – 75.00
REMARKS: From the collection of Cheryl & Joel Knolmayer.

PLATE: 183
HEIGHT: 6½"
COLOR: Chartreuse
STYLE: Pitcher
HANDLE: Drop Over
COMPANY: Pilgrim
DATE: 1960s
VALUE: $60.00 – 65.00

PLATE: 184
HEIGHT: 6¾"
COLOR: Amberina
STYLE: Pitcher
HANDLE: Drop Over
COMPANY: Rainbow
DATE: 1940s – 1960s
VALUE: $75.00 – 85.00

PLATE: 185
HEIGHT: 7"
COLOR: Yellow
STYLE: Pitcher
HANDLE: Pulled Back
COMPANY: Kanawha
DATE: 1957 – 1987
VALUE: $70.00 – 80.00

PLATE: 187
HEIGHT: 7¾
COLOR: Amberina
STYLE: Pitcher
HANDLE: Drop Over
COMPANY: New England Glass Company
DATE: 1880s
VALUE: $600.00 – 700.00
REMARKS: This exact pitcher is displayed in the
           Milan Historical Museum.

PLATE 187A. Inset of Plate 187.

ATE: 186
IGHT: 7"
)LOR: Crystal
YLE: Pitcher
NDLE: Pulled Back
)MPANY: Kanawha
TE: 1957 – 1987
LUE: $75.00 – 85.00
MARKS: From the collection
         of Dennis & Joan Davis.

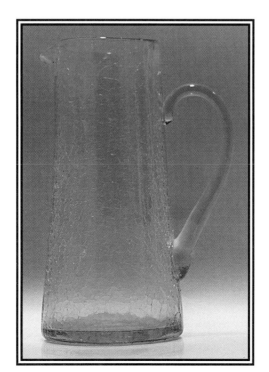

PLATE: 188
HEIGHT: 7¼"
COLOR: Vaseline Yellow
STYLE: Pitcher
HANDLE: Drop Over
COMPANY: Pilgrim
DATE: 1949 – 1969
VALUE: $70.00 – 80.00

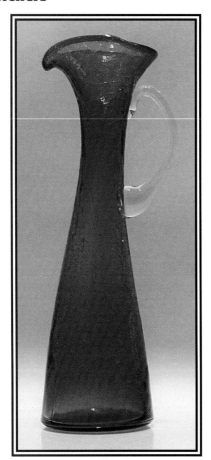

PLATE: 189
HEIGHT: 7¾"
COLOR: Cranberry
STYLE: Pitcher
HANDLE: Drop Over
COMPANY: Kanawha
DATE: 1957 – 1987
VALUE: $100.00 – 125.00

PLATE: 190
HEIGHT: 8"
COLOR: Topaz
STYLE: Pitcher
HANDLE: Drop Over
COMPANY: Kanawha
DATE: 1957 – 1987
VALUE: $75.00 – 80.00

PLATE: 191
HEIGHT: 8"
COLOR: Crystal with Enamel Work
STYLE: Pitcher
HANDLE: Crystal Drop Over
COMPANY: Unknown (Probably European)
DATE: Unknown
VALUE: $200.00 – 300.00
REMARKS: Mold blown. Courtesy of Steven
& Helen Klemko.

PLATE: 192
HEIGHT: 8"
COLOR: Emerald Green
STYLE: Pitcher
HANDLE: Crystal Drop Over
COMPANY: Bischoff
DATE: 1950s
VALUE: $75.00 – 85.00
REMARKS: Note big chunk of
           concrete in handle.

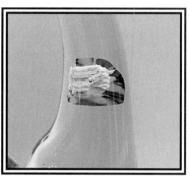

PLATE 192A.
Inset of Plate 192.

PLATE: 193
HEIGHT: 8¼"
COLOR: Emerald Green
STYLE: Pitcher
HANDLE: Pulled Back
COMPANY: Unknown
DATE: Unknown
VALUE: $80.00 – 90.00
REMARKS: Send us your thoughts on this
           piece concerning the ship motif.

PLATE: 194
HEIGHT: 8½"
COLOR: Topaz
STYLE: Pitcher
HANDLE: Pulled Back
COMPANY: Rainbow
DATE: 1940s – 1960s
VALUE: $80.00 – 90.00

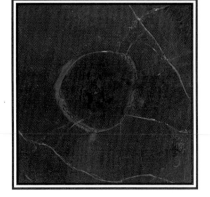

PLATE 196A. Inset of Plate 196.

PLATE: 195
HEIGHT: 9"
COLOR: Yellow
STYLE: Pitcher
HANDLE: Drop Over
COMPANY: Rainbow
DATE: 1940s – 1960s
VALUE: $80.00 – 90.00

PLATE: 196
HEIGHT: 8¾"
COLOR: Amberina
STYLE: Pitcher
HANDLE: Drop Over
COMPANY: Blenko
DATE: 1960s
VALUE: $85.00 – 95.0
REMARKS: Red pontil.

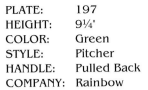

PLATE: 197
HEIGHT: 9¼"
COLOR: Green
STYLE: Pitcher
HANDLE: Pulled Back
COMPANY: Rainbow
DATE: 1940s – 1960s
VALUE: $80.00 – 90.00

PLATE: 198
HEIGHT: 9¼" (Glasses: 5¾")
COLOR: Topaz
STYLE: Pitcher Set
HANDLE: Drop Over
COMPANY: Unknown
DATE: Unknown
VALUE: Pitcher: $80.00 – 90.00
             Glasses: $25.00 – 35.00
REMARKS: Mold blown.

PLATE: 199
HEIGHT: 10"
COLOR: Orange
STYLE: Pitcher
HANDLE: Black Drop Over
COMPANY: Made in Czechoslovakia
VALUE: $125.00 – 150.00
REMARKS: From the collection of
             Cheryl & Joel Knolmayer.

PLATE: 200
HEIGHT: 10"
COLOR: Tangerine/Amberina
STYLE: Pitcher
HANDLE: Drop Over
COMPANY: Blenko
DATE: 1973
VALUE: $80.00 – 110.00

PLATE: 201
HEIGHT: 11"
COLOR: Topaz
STYLE: Pitcher
HANDLE: Drop Over
COMPANY: Bischoff
DATE: 1940 – 1963
VALUE: $80.00 – 110.00
REMARKS: From the collection of
          Cheryl & Joel Knolmayer.

PLATE: 202
HEIGHT: 11"
COLOR: Tangerine
STYLE: Pitcher
HANDLE: Crystal Drop Over
COMPANY: Blenko
DATE: 1960s
VALUE: $90.00 – 110.00
REMARKS: From the collection of
          Cheryl & Joel Knolmayer.

PLATE: 203
HEIGHT: 11"
COLOR: Crystal
STYLE: Water Pitcher
HANDLE: Drop Over
COMPANY: Possibly European
DATE: Unknown
VALUE: $125.00 – 150.00
REMARKS: Polished pontil.

PLATE: 204
HEIGHT: 12"
COLOR: Crystal
STYLE: Pitcher Set
HANDLE: Drop Over
COMPANY: Possibly Pilgrim
DATE: 1949 – 1969
VALUE: Pitcher: $90.00 – 110.00
            Glasses: $25.00 – 35.00 each

PLATE: 205
HEIGHT: 12½"
COLOR: Gold
STYLE: Pitcher
HANDLE: Drop Over
COMPANY: Rainbow
DATE: 1960s
VALUE: $90.00 – 110.00

PLATE: 206
HEIGHT: 12¾"
COLOR: Crystal
STYLE: Giant Pitcher
HANDLE: Blue Drop Over
COMPANY: Blenko
DATE: 1960s
VALUE: $125.00 – 150.00

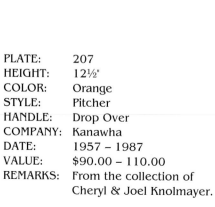

PLATE: 207
HEIGHT: 12½"
COLOR: Orange
STYLE: Pitcher
HANDLE: Drop Over
COMPANY: Kanawha
DATE: 1957 – 1987
VALUE: $90.00 – 110.00
REMARKS: From the collection of
            Cheryl & Joel Knolmayer.

PLATE: 208
HEIGHT: 13"
COLOR: Crystal with Lime Tint
STYLE: Pitcher
HANDLE: Pulled Back
COMPANY: Unknown
DATE: Unknown
VALUE: $110.00 – 135.00

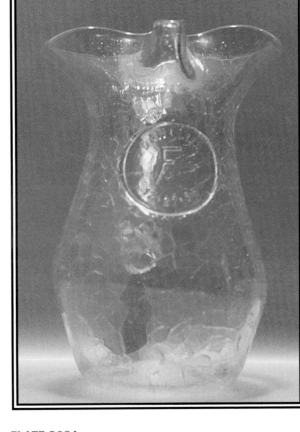

PLATE 208A.
Front view of Plate 208.

PLATE 208B.
Inset of of Plate 208A.

PLATE: 209
HEIGHT: 13"
COLOR: Blue
STYLE: Pitcher
HANDLE: Drop Over
COMPANY: Rainbow
DATE: 1958
VALUE: $110.00 – 125.00

PLATE: 210
HEIGHT: 13"
COLOR: Orange
STYLE: Pitcher
HANDLE: Drop Over
COMPANY: Blenko
DATE: 1960s
VALUE: $110.00 – 135.00

PLATE: 211
HEIGHT: 13½"
COLOR: Amethyst
STYLE: Pitcher
HANDLE: Drop Over
COMPANY: Pilgrim
DATE: 1949 – 1969
VALUE: $125.00 – 150.00

PLATE: 212
HEIGHT: 14"
COLOR: Emerald Green
STYLE: Pitcher
HANDLE: Pulled Back
COMPANY: Bischoff
DATE: 1950s
VALUE: $125.00 – 150.00
REMARKS: Unique shape. From the
collection of Cheryl & Joel
Knolmayer.

Decanters

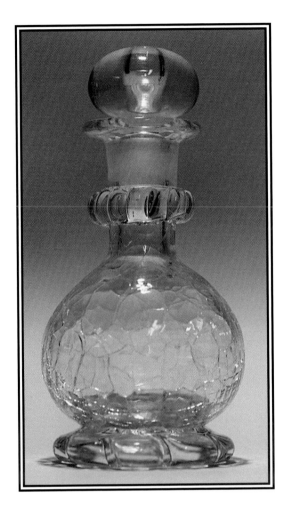

PLATE: 213
HEIGHT: 6¼"
COLOR: Crystal
STYLE: Decanter
COMPANY: Bonita
DATE: 1931 – 1953
VALUE: $85.00 – 100.00
REMARKS: From the collection of
Cheryl & Joel Knolmayer.

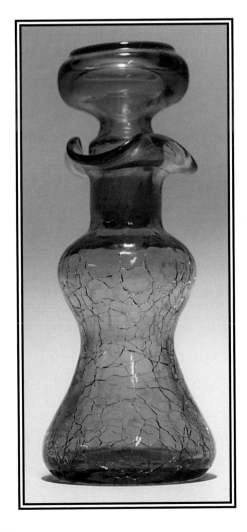

PLATE: 214
HEIGHT: 6½"
COLOR: Blue
STYLE: Cruet
COMPANY: Rainbow
DATE: 1940s – 1960s
VALUE: $85.00 – 100.00
REMARKS: From the collection of
Cheryl & Joel Knolmayer.

PLATE: 215
HEIGHT: 7"
COLOR: Amber
STYLE: Decanter
COMPANY: Czechoslovakian
DATE: 1920s
VALUE: $125.00 – 150.00
REMARKS: Note enamel work.

PLATE 215A.
Side view of Plate 215.

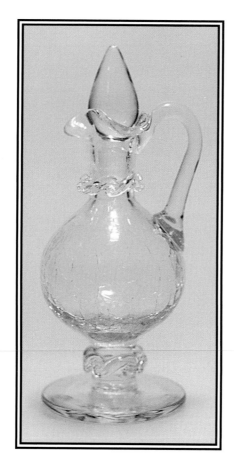

PLATE: 216
HEIGHT: 7"
COLOR: Crystal
STYLE: Decanter
HANDLE: Drop Over
COMPANY: Bonita
DATE: 1931 – 1953
VALUE: $85.00 – 100.00
REMARKS: From the collection of
           Dennis & Joan Davis.

PLATE: 217
HEIGHT: 7¼"
COLOR: Crystal
STYLE: Decanter
COMPANY: Unknown
DATE: Unknown
VALUE: $50.00 – 75.00

PLATE: 218
HEIGHT: 7¾"
COLOR: Amberina
STYLE: Decanter
COMPANY: Rainbow
DATE: 1940s – 1960s
VALUE: $100.00 – 125.00

PLATE: 219
HEIGHT: 7¼"
COLOR: Amber
STYLE: Decanter
COMPANY: Probably European
DATE: Early 1900s
VALUE: $250.00 – 350.00
REMARKS: Polished pontil. From the collection of
          Cheryl & Joel Knolmayer.

PLATE: 220
HEIGHT: 7¾"
COLOR: Blue
STYLE: Decanter
COMPANY: Rainbow
DATE: 1940s – 1960s
VALUE: $85.00 – 100.00

PLATE: 221
HEIGHT: 8¼"
COLOR: Orange
STYLE: Decanter
DATE: 1940s – 1960s
VALUE: $85.00 – 100.00
REMARKS: From the collection of
           Cheryl & Joel Knolmayer.

PLATE: 222
HEIGHT: 8" (10" across)
COLOR: Ruby
STYLE: Captain's Decanter
COMPANY: Pilgrim
DATE: 1949 – 1969
VALUE: $200.00 – 225.00

PLATE: 223
HEIGHT: 8¼"
COLOR: Amber
STYLE: Decanter
COMPANY: Probably European
DATE: Early 1900s
VALUE: $250.00 – 350.00
REMARKS: Polished pontil. From the
           collection of Cheryl & Joel Knolmayer.

PLATE: 224
HEIGHT: 8½"
COLOR: Amethyst
STYLE: Decanter
COMPANY: Rainbow
DATE: 1940s – 1960s
VALUE: $100.00 – 125.00
REMARKS: Amethyst demands a higher price.
           From the collection of Cheryl &
           Joel Knolmayer.

PLATE: 225
HEIGHT: 9¾"
COLOR: Emerald Green
STYLE: Pinched Decanter
HANDLE: Drop Over
COMPANY: Bischoff
DATE: 1950s
VALUE: $85.00 – 110.00

Decanters

PLATE: 226
HEIGHT: 8¾"
COLOR: Crystal with Enamel Work
STYLE: Decanter
COMPANY: Unknown
DATE: 1920s
VALUE: $125.00 – 150.00
REMARKS: Made in Czechoslovakia.
Courtesy of Dorothy Watkins, Evans, Georgia.

PLATE 226A. Inset of Plate 226.

PLATE: 227
HEIGHT: N/A
COLOR: Amethyst
STYLE: Decanter
COMPANY: Blenko
DATE: 1930
VALUE: N/A
REMARKS: Courtesy of the Blenko Glass
Company Museum.

PLATE: 228
HEIGHT: 10"
COLOR: Iridescent Crystal with Amethyst Stopper
STYLE: Captain's Decanter
COMPANY: Hamon
DATE: Late 1940s – 1970s
VALUE: $300.00 – 400.00
REMARKS: Widest measurement at the base is 14".

PLATE: 229
HEIGHT: 10½"
COLOR: Cranberry Flash
STYLE: Decanter
COMPANY: Unknown
DATE: Unknown
VALUE: $250.00 – 300.00
REMARKS: Unusual stopper. From the
collection of Dennis &
Joan Davis.

PLATE: 230
HEIGHT: 10¾"
COLOR: Blue
STYLE: Decanter
COMPANY: Blenko
DATE: 1940s – 1950s
VALUE: $100.00 – 125.00

PLATE: 231
HEIGHT: 6½"
COLOR: Crystal with Enamel Work
STYLE: Decanter
COMPANY: European
DATE: 1920s
VALUE: $150.00 – 200.00
REMARKS: From the collection of
            Dennis & Joan Davis.

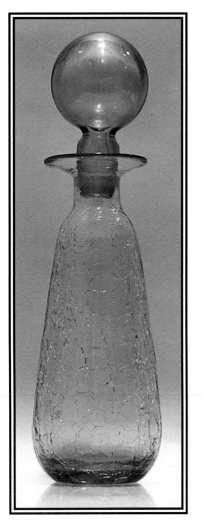

PLATE: 232
HEIGHT: Decanter: 11"; Glasses: 2"
COLOR: Crystal
STYLE: Decanter & Glasses
COMPANY: Made in Czechoslovakia
DATE: Unknown
VALUE: $225.00 – 250.00 for the set

PLATE: 233
HEIGHT: 11"
COLOR: Topaz
STYLE: Decanter
COMPANY: Rainbow
DATE: 1953
VALUE: $100.00 – 125.00

PLATE: 234
HEIGHT: 11"
COLOR: Smoke Gray
STYLE: Decanter
COMPANY: Pilgrim
DATE: 1950s
VALUE: $100.00 – 125.00
REMARKS: Smoke gray warrants a higher
           value, as it was only in the production
           line for a short time in the 1950s.

PLATE: 235
HEIGHT: 11"
COLOR: Blue
STYLE: Decanter
COMPANY: Pilgrim
DATE: 1949 – 1969
VALUE: $85.00 – 100.00

PLATE: 236
HEIGHT: 11" & 11⅛"
COLOR: Crystal
STYLE: Decanters
COMPANY: Pilgrim
DATE: 1949 – 1969
VALUE: $85.00 – 100.00 each

PLATE: 237
HEIGHT: 11¼"
COLOR: Topaz
STYLE: Decanter
COMPANY: Czechoslovakia
DATE: 1920 – 1930
VALUE: $150.00 – 200.00
REMARKS: From the collections of
           Cheryl & Joel Knolmayer.

PLATE: 238
HEIGHT: 11¼"
COLOR: Crystal with Blue Stopper
STYLE: Pinched Decanter
COMPANY: Blenko
DATE: 1940s – 1950s
VALUE: $100.00 – 125.00

PLATE: 239
HEIGHT: 11½" (Cups: 1½")
COLOR: Dark Blue
STYLE: Decanter
COMPANY: Unknown
DATE: Unknown
VALUE: Decanter: $200.00 – 250.00
           Cups: $50.00 – 65.00 each
REMARKS: Decoration is pewter.

PLATE: 240
HEIGHT: 11½"
COLOR: Crystal
STYLE: Decanter
COMPANY: Made in Czechoslovakia
DATE: Unknown
VALUE: $185.00 – 250.00
REMARKS: Original box and label unbroken.

PLATE: 241
HEIGHT: 11½"
COLOR: Crystal
STYLE: Decanter
COMPANY: Blenko
DATE: 1950s
VALUE: $100.00 – 125.00

PLATE: 242
HEIGHT: 11½"
COLOR: Blue
STYLE: Decanter
HANDLE: Drop Over
COMPANY: Blenko (Designer: Winslow Anderson)
DATE: Late 1940s
VALUE: $125.00 – 150.00
REMARKS: From the collection of Cheryl & Joel Knolmayer.

PLATE: 243
HEIGHT: 11½"
COLOR: Crystal to Green
STYLE: Pitcher
HANDLE: Brass
COMPANY: Probably European
DATE: Unknown
VALUE: $175.00 – 225.00

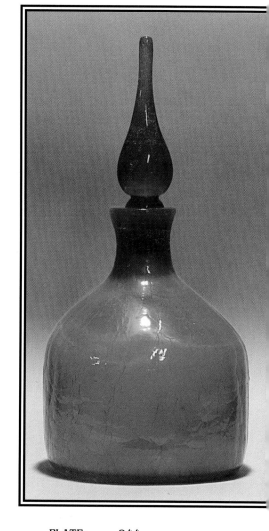

PLATE: 244
HEIGHT: 11¾"
COLOR: Butterscotch
STYLE: Decanter
COMPANY: Rainbow
DATE: 1950s
VALUE: $175.00 – 200.00
REMARKS: Unique color. From the
            collection of Cheryl & Joel
            Knolmayer.

PLATE: 245
HEIGHT: 12"
COLOR: Amber
STYLE: Water Pitcher
HANDLE: Blue Drop Over
COMPANY: Unknown
DATE: Unknown
VALUE: $175.00 – 200.00
REMARKS: Look how the two colors complement each other.
            From the collection of Cheryl & Joel Knolmayer.

PLATE: 246
HEIGHT: 12"
COLOR: Emerald Green
STYLE: Decanter
COMPANY: Rainbow
DATE: 1940s – 1960s
VALUE: $150.00 – 175.00.
REMARKS: Updated price from first book. Paper label courtesy of
            Wally Davis, Fall River, Mass.

PLATE 246A. Inset of Plate 246.

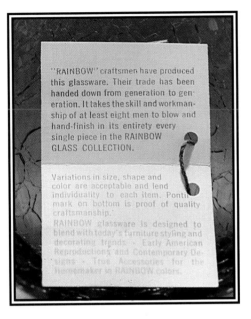

"RAINBOW" craftsmen have produced
this glassware. Their trade has been
handed down from generation to generation. It takes the skill and workman-
ship of at least eight men to blow and
hand-finish in its entirety every
single piece in the RAINBOW
GLASS COLLECTION.

Variations in size, shape and
color are acceptable and lend
individuality to each item. Pontil
mark on bottom is proof of quality
craftsmanship.'
RAINBOW glassware is designed to
blend with today's furniture styling and
decorating trends. - Early American
Reproductions and Contemporary Designs - True Accessories for the
homemaker in RAINBOW colors.

PLATE 246B. Inset of Plate 246.

PLATE: 247
HEIGHT: 13"
COLOR: Blue
STYLE: Decanter
HANDLE: Pulled Back
COMPANY: Hamon
DATE: 1966 – 1970s
VALUE: $150.00 – 175.00
REMARKS: Hamon and Kanawha merged in 1966. This is a Hamon
            piece even though it has a Kanawha label. From the
            collection of Cheryl & Joel Knolmayer.

PLATE: 248
HEIGHT: Decanter: 13½"; Glasses: 2¼"
COLOR: Crystal with Rosettes
STYLE: Decanter Set
COMPANY: Blenko
DATE: 1938
VALUE: Decanter: $250.00 – 275.00
           Glasses: $50.00 – 75.00 each

PLATE 248A. Close-up of glass.

PLATE 248B. Close-up of decanter, stopper & rosettes.

PLATE: 249
HEIGHT: 13¾"
COLOR: Green
STYLE: Captain's Decanter
COMPANY: Blenko
DATE: 1965
VALUE: $150.00 – 175.00
REMARKS: From the collection of Cheryl & Joel Knolmayer.

PLATE: 251
HEIGHT: 13¾"
COLOR: Amberina
STYLE: Decanter
COMPANY: Rainbow
DATE: 1940s – 1960s
VALUE: $150.00 – 175.00

PLATE: 250
HEIGHT: 13½"
COLOR: Crystal
STYLE: Decanter
HANDLE: Emerald Green Drop Over
COMPANY: Bischoff
DATE: 1940 – 1963
VALUE: $150.00 – 175.00

PLATE: 252
HEIGHT: 14¾"
COLOR: Blue
STYLE: Decanter
COMPANY: Blenko
DATE: 1965
VALUE: $150.00 – 175.00
REMARKS: Amethyst is a highly
            collectible color and
            warrants a higher price.

PLATE: 253
HEIGHT: 15"
COLOR: Crystal with Blue Stopper
            & Trim
STYLE: Decanter
COMPANY: Rainbow
DATE: 1950s
VALUE: $150.00 – 175.00
REMARKS: From the collection of
            Cheryl & Joel
            Knolmayer.

PLATE: 254
HEIGHT: 15¼"
COLOR: Amethyst
STYLE: Decanter
COMPANY: Rainbow
DATE: 1958
VALUE: $175.00 – 200.00
REMARKS: Amethyst is a highly
            collectible color and
            warrants a higher price.

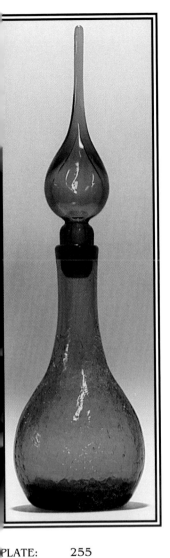

PLATE: 255
HEIGHT: 15¼"
COLOR: Aquamarine
STYLE: Decanter
COMPANY: Rainbow
DATE: 1950s
VALUE: $150.00 – 175.00
REMARKS: From the collection of
            Cheryl & Joel
            Knolmayer.

PLATE: 256
HEIGHT: 15½"
COLOR: Ruby
STYLE: Decanter
COMPANY: Pilgrim
DATE: 1947 – 1967
VALUE: $160.00 – 185.00

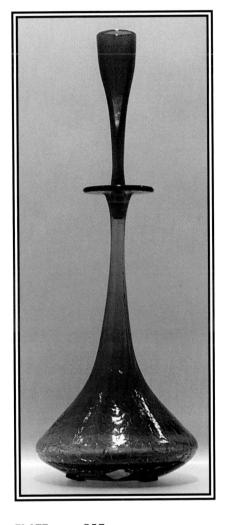

PLATE: 257
HEIGHT: 16¼"
COLOR: Amethyst
STYLE: Decanter
COMPANY: Blenko
DATE: 1960
VALUE: $175.00 – 250.00
REMARKS: Note the stopper is
            also a glass. Note tag
            on bottom of bottle.
            This is the original
            store tag from the
            Blenko Gift Shop.

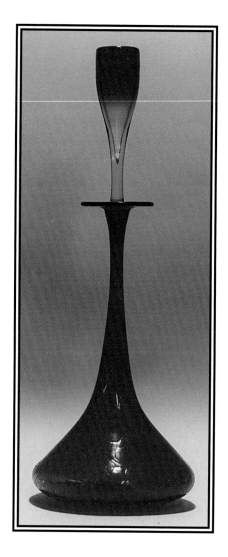

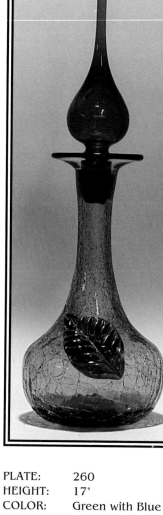

PLATE: 258
HEIGHT: 17"
COLOR: Amberina
STYLE: Decanter
COMPANY: Blenko
DATE: 1961
VALUE: $175.00 – 200.00
REMARKS: From the collection of
           Cheryl & Joel Knolmayer.

PLATE: 260
HEIGHT: 17"
COLOR: Green with Blue
           Stopper & Blue Lea
STYLE: Decanter
COMPANY: Rainbow
DATE: 1940s – 1960s
VALUE: $175.00 – 200.00
REMARKS: From the collectior
           of Cheryl & Joel
           Knolmayer.

PLATE: 259
HEIGHT: 16½"
COLOR: Amethyst
STYLE: Decanter
COMPANY: Probably Rainbow
DATE: 1940s – 1960s
VALUE: $150.00 – 200.00
REMARKS: Amethyst is a highly collectible
           color and warrants a higher price.

PLATE: 261
HEIGHT: 17"
COLOR: Crystal
STYLE: Decanter
COMPANY: Rainbow
DATE: 1940s – 1960s
VALUE: $175.00 – 200.00

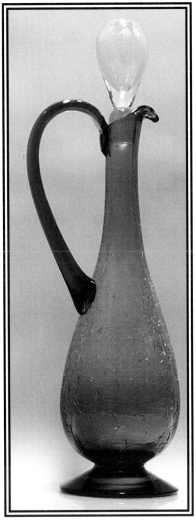

PLATE 261A. Inset of Plate 261.

PLATE: 262
HEIGHT: 17¼"
COLOR: Amethyst
STYLE: Decanter
HANDLE: Drop Over
COMPANY: Bischoff
DATE: 1950s
VALUE: $175.00 – 250.00
REMARKS: This decanter is signed
on the bottom "VIVANI."
Amethyst is a highly
collectible color and
warrants a higher price.

PLATE: 263
HEIGHT: 17¼"
COLOR: Olive Green
STYLE: Decanter
COMPANY: Pilgrim
DATE: 1949 – 1969
VALUE: $150.00 – 175.00

PLATE: 264
HEIGHT: 18"
COLOR: Amethyst
STYLE: Decanter
COMPANY: Rainbow
DATE: 1940s – 1960s
VALUE: $175.00 – 250.00
REMARKS: Amethyst is a highly collectible color and warrants a higher price.

PLATE: 265
HEIGHT: 12¼"
COLOR: Olive Green and Blue
STYLE: Decanter
COMPANY: Rainbow
DATE: 1940s – 1960s
VALUE: $175.00 – 200.00
REMARKS: From the collection of Dennis & Joan Davis.

PLATE: 266
HEIGHT: 24"
COLOR: Yellow
STYLE: Decanter
COMPANY: Blenko
DATE: 1960s
VALUE: $200.00 – 250.00
REMARKS: From the collection of
Dennis & Joan Davis.

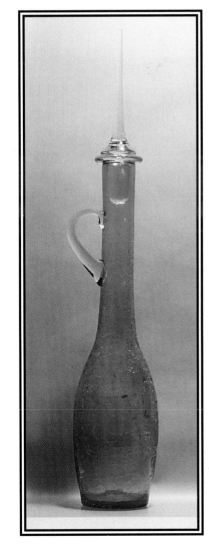

PLATE: 267
HEIGHT: 35"
COLOR: Blue
STYLE: Decanter
HANDLE: Drop Over
COMPANY: Bischoff
DATE: 1940 – 1963
VALUE: $275.00 – 350.00
REMARKS: We call the stopper the
Empire State Top. It looks
like the top of the Empire
State Building.

PLATE: 268
HEIGHT: 5"
COLOR: Green
STYLE: Jug
HANDLE: Drop Over
COMPANY: Jamestown
DATE: Late 1950s – 1968
VALUE: $50.00 – 55.00

PLATE: 269
HEIGHT: 6"
COLOR: Topaz
STYLE: Jug
HANDLE: Drop Over
COMPANY: Pilgrim
DATE: 1949 – 1969
VALUE: $60.00 – 65.00

PLATE: 270
HEIGHT: 6½"
COLOR: Amber
STYLE: Jug
HANDLE: Drop Over
COMPANY: Rainbow
DATE: 1940s – 1960s
VALUE: $65.00 – 70.00

PLATE: 271
HEIGHT: 17½"
COLOR: Crystal
STYLE: Jug
HANDLE: Green Drop Over
COMPANY: Bischoff
DATE: 1950s
VALUE: $125.00 – 150.00
REMARKS: From the collection
           of Cheryl & Joel
           Knolmayer.

PLATE: 272
HEIGHT: 7"
COLOR: Amberina
STYLE: Jug
HANDLE: Drop Over
COMPANY: Pilgrim
DATE: 1949 – 1969
VALUE: $65.00 – 70.00

PLATE: 273
HEIGHT: 4"
COLOR: Rose Crystal
STYLE: Cruet
HANDLE: Drop Over
COMPANY: Unknown
DATE: Unknown
VALUE: $75.00 – 100.00
REMARKS: From the collection of Cheryl & Joel Knolmayer.

PLATE 274A. Inset of Plate 274.

PLATE: 274
HEIGHT: 4½"
COLOR: Light Teal
STYLE: Cruet
COMPANY: Germany
DATE: 1972
VALUE: $125.00 – 150.00 (Pair)
REMARKS: Dated under copper stopper.

PLATE: 275
HEIGHT: 5½"
COLOR: Topaz
STYLE: Cruets
HANDLE: Pulled Back
COMPANY: Pilgrim
DATE: 1949 – 1969
VALUE: $110.00 – 150.00 (Pair)

PLATE: 276
HEIGHT: 6"
COLOR: Crystal
STYLE: Cruet
HANDLE: Pulled Back
COMPANY: Hamon
DATE: 1940s – 1966
VALUE: $50.00 – 75.00

PLATE: 277
HEIGHT: 6½"
COLOR: Blue
STYLE: Cruet
HANDLE: Drop Over
COMPANY: Rainbow
DATE: 1940s – 1960s
VALUE: $50.00 – 75.00

PLATE: 278
HEIGHT: 6½"
COLOR: Blue
STYLE: Cruet
HANDLE: Pulled Back
COMPANY: Hamon/Kanawha Catalog
DATE: 1940s – 1970s
VALUE: $50.00 – 75.00

PLATE: 279
HEIGHT: 6¼"
COLOR: Blue
STYLE: Cruet
HANDLE: Pulled Back
COMPANY: Pilgrim
DATE: 1949 – 1969
VALUE: $50.00 – 75.00

PLATE: 280
HEIGHT: 6¾"
COLOR: Orange
STYLE: Cruet
HANDLE: Pulled Back
COMPANY: Rainbow
DATE: 1940s – 1960s
VALUE: $65.00 – 85.00
REMARKS: Bell shape.

PLATE: 281
HEIGHT: 6¾
COLOR: Blue
STYLE: Cruet
HANDLE: Pulled Back
COMPANY: Pilgrim
DATE: 1949 – 1969
VALUE: $50.00 – 75.00
REMARKS: Very thin and fragile handle.

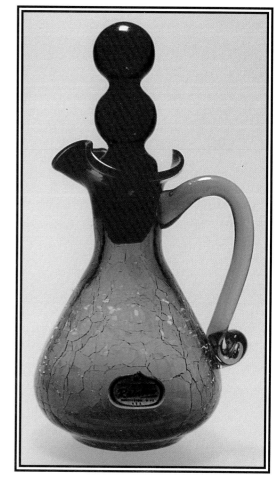

PLATE: 282
HEIGHT: 6¾"
COLOR: Amberina
STYLE: Cruet
HANDLE: Pulled Back
COMPANY: Rainbow
DATE: 1940s – 1960s
VALUE: $65.00 – 85.00
REMARKS: From the collection of
            Dennis & Joan Davis.

PLATE: 283
HEIGHT: 7"
COLOR: Amethyst
STYLE: Cruet
HANDLE: Pulled Back
COMPANY: Rainbow
DATE: 1940s – 1960s
VALUE: $75.00 – 100.00
REMARKS: Amethyst is a highly
            collectible color and
            warrants a higher price.

PLATE: 284
HEIGHT: 7"
COLOR: Blue
STYLE: Cruet
HANDLE: Pulled Back
COMPANY: Rainbow
DATE: 1940s – 1960s
VALUE: $55.00 – 80.00

PLATE: 286
HEIGHT: 8½
COLOR: Crystal
STYLE: Cruets
HANDLE: Drop Over
COMPANY: Bonita
DATE: 1931 – 1953
VALUE: $200.00 – 250.00 (Pair)
REMARKS: From the collection of Cheryl &
            Joel Knolmayer.

PLATE: 285
HEIGHT: 7¼"
COLOR: Amberina
STYLE: Syrup
HANDLE: Drop Over
COMPANY: Kanawha
DATE: 1957 – 1987
VALUE: $60.00 – 70.00

Bowls and Dishes

PLATE: 287
HEIGHT: 2½"
ACROSS: 4½"
COLOR: Sea Green
STYLE: Miniature Bowl
COMPANY: Blenko
DATE: 1950s – 1960s
VALUE: $50.00 – 75.00
REMARKS: From the collection of
           Cheryl & Joel Knolmayer.

PLATE: 288
HEIGHT: 2¾"
ACROSS: 4½"
COLOR: Amber
STYLE: Bowl
COMPANY: Kanawha
DATE: 1957 – 1987
VALUE: $40.00 – 45.00

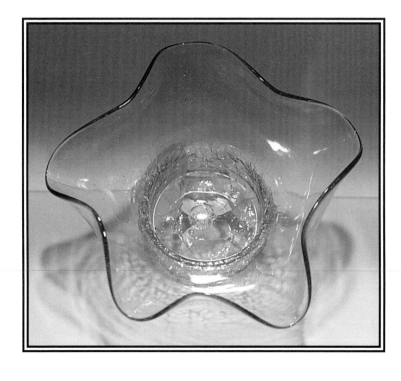

PLATE: 289
HEIGHT: 2½"
ACROSS: 5½"
COLOR: Light Blue
STYLE: Scalloped Bowl
COMPANY: Blenko
DATE: 1960s
VALUE: $45.00 – 55.00

PLATE: 290
HEIGHT: 3"
ACROSS: 5"
COLOR: Amberina
STYLE: Candy Dish
COMPANY: Kanawha
DATE: 1957 – 1987
VALUE: $45.00 – 55.00

PLATE: 291
HEIGHT: 3"
ACROSS: 4½"
COLOR: Green
STYLE: Candy Dish
COMPANY: Kanawha
DATE: 1957 – 1987
VALUE: $45.00 – 55.00
REMARKS: Labels increase
the price.

PLATE: 292
HEIGHT: 3"
ACROSS: 3¼"
COLOR: Crystal
STYLE: Nappy
COMPANY: Unknown
DATE: Unknown
VALUE: $45.00 – 55.00

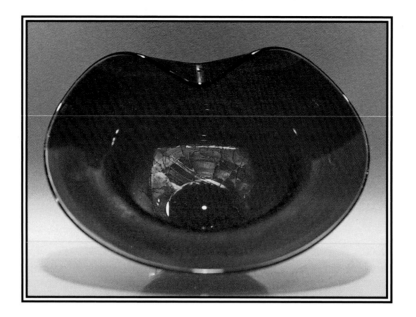

PLATE: 293
HEIGHT: 2½"
ACROSS: 3¼"
COLOR: Amberina
STYLE: Nappy
COMPANY: Rainbow/Bischoff
DATE: 1940s – 1960s/1942 – 1963
VALUE: $50.00 – 75.00

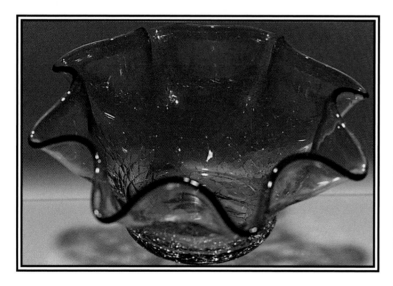

PLATE: 294
HEIGHT: 3"
ACROSS: 3½"
COLOR: Green
STYLE: Candy Dish
COMPANY: Bischoff
DATE: 1942 – 1963
VALUE: $45.00 – 55.00

PLATE: 295
HEIGHT: 5"
ACROSS: 3"
COLOR: Topaz
STYLE: Patio Light
COMPANY: Viking
DATE: 1944 – 1960
VALUE: $40.00 – 50.00

PLATE: 296
HEIGHT: 2¾"
ACROSS: 3¼"
COLOR: Ruby
STYLE: Heart-shape Bowl (Bonbon)
HANDLE: Yellow
COMPANY: Rainbow, Viking, and/or
          Kanawha
DATE: 1950 – 1960s
VALUE: $55.00 – 85.00

PLATE: 297
HEIGHT: 4½"
ACROSS: 5"
COLOR: Tangerine/Amberina
STYLE: Rose Bowl
COMPANY: Blenko
DATE: 1960s
VALUE: $100.00 – 125.00

PLATE: 298
HEIGHT: 5"
ACROSS: 4½"
COLOR: Topaz
STYLE: Rose Bowl
COMPANY: Blenko
DATE: 1950 – 1960
VALUE: $95.00 – 110.00
REMARKS: Large cracks.

PLATE: 299
HEIGHT: 4½"
COLOR: Crystal
STYLE: Stemmed Bowl
HANDLE: Red
COMPANY: Czechoslovakia
DATE: Late 1800s
VALUE: $250.00 – 325.00
REMARKS: From the collection of Dennis & Joan Davis.

PLATE: 300
HEIGHT: 5"
ACROSS: 4"
COLOR: Crystal
STYLE: Ice Bucket
HANDLE: White Metal
COMPANY: Unknown
DATE: Unknown
VALUE: $75.00 – 100.00

PLATE: 301
HEIGHT: 5"
ACROSS: 4½"
COLOR: Crystal
STYLE: Ice Bucket
HANDLE: Metal
COMPANY: Unknown
DATE: Unknown
VALUE: $75.00 – 100.00

PLATE: 302
HEIGHT: 5"
ACROSS: 6"
COLOR: Lemon Drop Yellow
STYLE: Handkerchief Bowl
COMPANY: Bischoff
DATE: 1942 – 1963
VALUE: $100.00 – 125.00
REMARKS: From the collection of
          Cheryl & Joel Knolmayer.

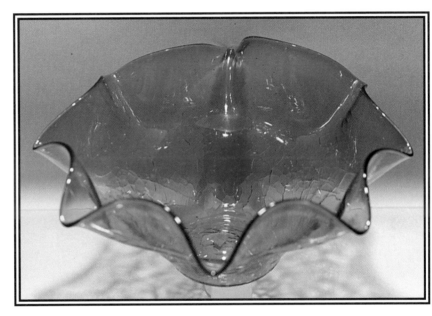

PLATE: 303
HEIGHT: 5"
ACROSS: 10¾"
COLOR: Blue
STYLE: Candy Dish
COMPANY: Bischoff
DATE: 1942 – 1963
VALUE: $75.00 – 100.00

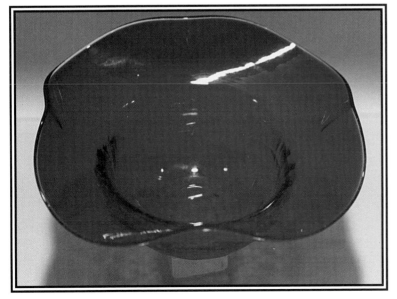

PLATE: 304
HEIGHT: 4½"
ACROSS: 5"
COLOR: Ruby
STYLE: Candy Dish
COMPANY: Bischoff
DATE: 1940 – 1963
VALUE: $55.00 – 85.00

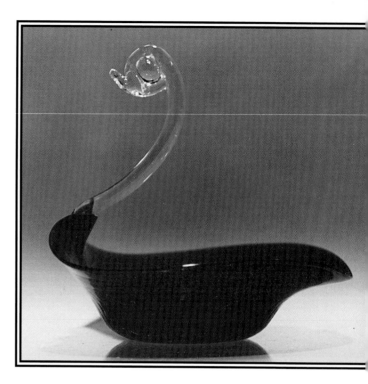

PLATE: 305
HEIGHT: 5¼"
ACROSS: 4½"
COLOR: Tangerine
STYLE: Rose Bowl
COMPANY: Pilgrim
DATE: 1949 – 1969
VALUE: $100.00 – 125.00
REMARKS: Very small cracks. Strawberry-looking
            mark on pontil. Only Pilgrim Glass
            Company used this technique for iden-
            tification. Remember: Not all Pilgrim
            pieces have this mark. See Book 1,
            Page 9 for further explanation.

PLATE: 306
HEIGHT: 6" x 7" x 5½"
COLOR: Orange
STYLE: Heart-shape Swan Dish
COMPANY: Kanawha
DATE: 1957 – 1987
VALUE: $75.00 – 100.00

PLATE: 307
HEIGHT: 6"
ACROSS: 6"
COLOR: Tangerine
STYLE: Compote
COMPANY: Blenko
DATE: 1950s
VALUE: $75.00 – 100.00
REMARKS: Courtesy of Bayvillage Gardens &
            Antiques, Amityville, Long Island.

PLATE: 308
HEIGHT: 6"
ACROSS: 8"
COLOR: Blue
STYLE: Rose Bowl
COMPANY: Blenko
DATE: 1950s
VALUE: $95.00 – 110.00

PLATE: 309
HEIGHT: 7"
COLOR: Crystal with Blue Foot
STYLE: Footed Bowl
COMPANY: Blenko
DATE: 1950s
VALUE: $100.00 – 125.00

PLATE: 310
HEIGHT: 8"
COLOR: Crystal with Sea Green Bottom
STYLE: Footed Bowl
COMPANY: Blenko
DATE: 1940s – 1950s
VALUE: $75.00 – 100.00

PLATE: 311
HEIGHT: 3"
ACROSS: 6"
COLOR: Topaz
STYLE: Candy Dish/Ashtray
COMPANY: Bischoff
DATE: 1942 – 1963
VALUE: $55.00 – 85.00

PLATE: 12
HEIGHT: 5½"
ACROSS: 8¼
COLOR: Fire Orange
STYLE: Large Centerpiece
Footed Bowl
COMPANY: Pilgrim
DATE: 1949 – 1969
VALUE: $125.00 – 150.00

PLATE: 313
HEIGHT: 4"
ACROSS: 8½"
COLOR: Crystal with
Turquoise Trim
STYLE: Dish
COMPANY: Blenko
DATE: 1950s
VALUE: $100.00 – 125.00
REMARKS: From the collec-
tion of Cheryl &
Joel Knolmayer.

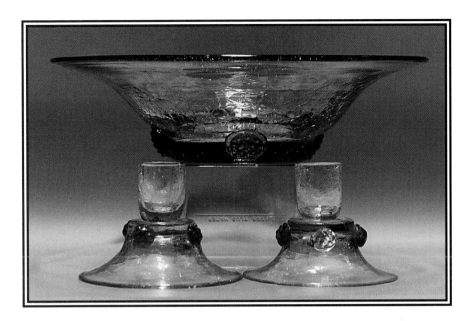

PLATE: 314
HEIGHT: Bowl: 4"; Candlestick Holders: 3½"
ACROSS: Bowl: 12"
COLOR: Crystal with Aquamarine Rosettes
STYLE: Compote Set
COMPANY: Blenko
DATE: 1942
VALUE: Bowl: $125.00 – 150.00; Candlestick Holders:
              $100.00 – 125.00 set

PLATE: 315
HEIGHT: 7½"
ACROSS: 6"
COLOR: Cranberry
STYLE: Ice Bucket
HANDLE: Metal
COMPANY: Unknown
DATE: Unknown
VALUE: $150.00 – 200.00
REMARKS: From the collection of Dennis
              & Joan Davis.

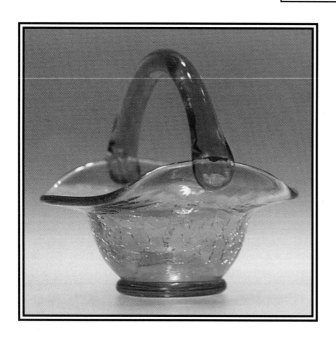

PLATE: 316
HEIGHT: 3¾"
COLOR: Blue
STYLE: Basket
HANDLE: Blue
COMPANY: Kanawha
DATE: 1957 – 1987
VALUE: $40.00 – 55.00

PLATE: 317
HEIGHT: 4¼"
COLOR: Olive Green
STYLE: Basket
HANDLE: Green
COMPANY: Kanawha
DATE: 1957 – 1987
VALUE: $40.00 – 55.00

PLATE: 318
HEIGHT: 4¾
COLOR: Orange
STYLE: Basket
HANDLE: Crystal
COMPANY: Hamon
DATE: 1940s – 1970s
VALUE: $50.00 – 75.00

PLATE: 319
HEIGHT: 4¾"
COLOR: Topaz
STYLE: Basket
HANDLE: Crystal
COMPANY: Pilgrim
DATE: 1960s
VALUE: $60.00 – 75.00
REMARKS: Labels increase price.

PLATE: 320
HEIGHT: 4¾"
COLOR: Amberina
STYLE: Basket
HANDLE: Crystal
COMPANY: Pilgrim
DATE: 1949 – 1969
VALUE: $50.00 – 75.00

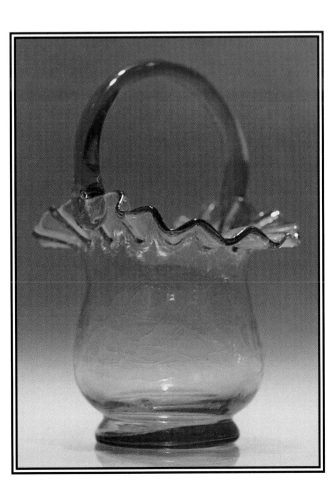

PLATE: 321
HEIGHT: 5"
COLOR: Topaz
STYLE: Basket
HANDLE: Topaz
COMPANY: Kanawha
DATE: 1957 – 1987
VALUE: $50.00 – 75.00

PLATE: 322
HEIGHT: 5¼"
COLOR: Topaz
STYLE: Basket
HANDLE: Crystal
COMPANY: Pilgrim
DATE: 1949 – 1969
VALUE: $50.00 – 75.00

PLATE: 323
HEIGHT: 5¼"
COLOR: Blue
STYLE: Basket
HANDLE: Crystal
COMPANY: Pilgrim
DATE: 1949 – 1969
VALUE: $50.00 – 75.00

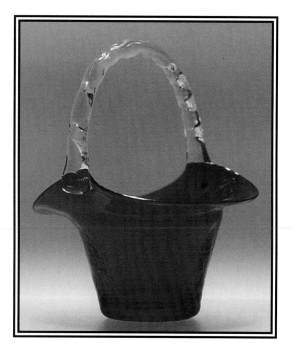

PLATE: 324
HEIGHT: 5¼"
COLOR: Ruby
STYLE: Basket
HANDLE: Twisted Crystal
COMPANY: Hamon/Kanawha
DATE: 1960s – 1970s
VALUE: $50.00 – 75.00
REMARKS: This basket was made by the Hamon Glass Company.
            Hamon and Kanawha merged in 1966. The basket is
            featured in some of the Kanawha catalogs. (For fur-
            ther information, see Book 1, Page 10.)

PLATE: 325
HEIGHT: 6"
COLOR: Ruby
STYLE: Basket
HANDLE: Crystal
COMPANY: Pilgrim
DATE: 1949 – 1969
VALUE: $50.00 – 75.00

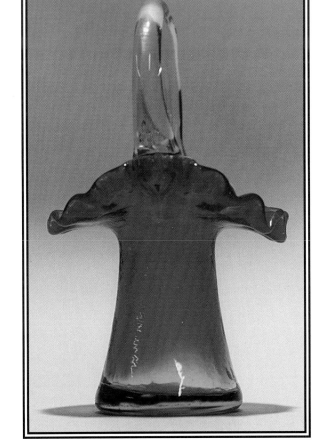

PLATE: 326
HEIGHT: 6"
COLOR: Amberina
STYLE: Basket
HANDLE: Crystal
COMPANY: Kanawha
DATE: 1957 – 1987
VALUE: $60.00 – 85.00
REMARKS: From the collection of
            Cheryl & Joel Knolmayer.

Glasses and Goblets

PLATE: 327
HEIGHT: 3½"
COLOR: Ruby
STYLE: Pinched Glass
COMPANY: Bischoff
DATE: 1950s
VALUE: $50.00 – 60.00

PLATE: 328
HEIGHT: 4"
COLOR: Crystal
STYLE: Glass
COMPANY: Unknown
DATE: Unknown
VALUE: $50.00 – 75.00
REMARKS: From the collection of
             Dennis & Joan Davis.

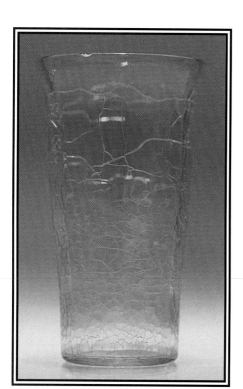

PLATE 329A.
Inset of Plate 329.

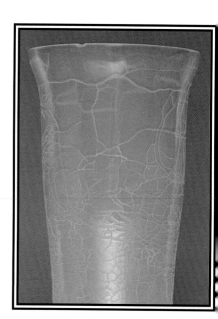

PLATE: 329
HEIGHT: 4"
COLOR: Green
STYLE: Juice Glass
COMPANY: Unknown
DATE: 1920s
VALUE: $25.00 – 30.00
REMARKS: Vaseline glass will
             fluoresce under black light.

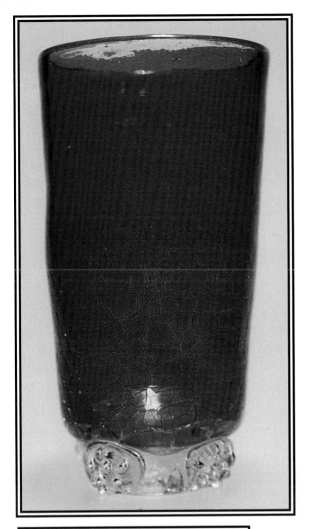

PLATE: 330
HEIGHT: 5½"
COLOR: Cranberry Flash
STYLE: Glass
COMPANY: Unknown
DATE: Unknown
VALUE: $75.00 – 100.00
REMARKS: From the collection of
           Dennis & Joan Davis.

PLATE: 331
HEIGHT: 5¾
COLOR: Crystal
STYLE: Glass
COMPANY: Blenko
DATE: 1950s
VALUE: $75.00 – 85.00

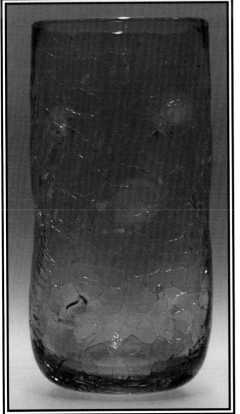

PLATE: 332
HEIGHT: 6"
COLOR: Blue/Green
STYLE: Pinched Glass
COMPANY: Blenko
DATE: 1940s – 1950s
VALUE: $55.00 – 75.00

PLATE: 333
HEIGHT: 7½
COLOR: Crystal
STYLE: Footed Goblet
COMPANY: Unknown
DATE: Unknown
VALUE: $50.00 – 75.00

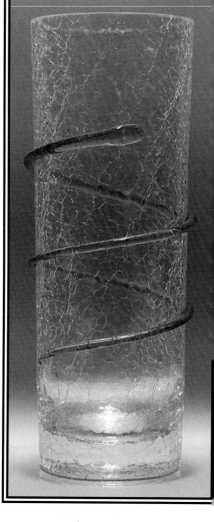

PLATE: 334
HEIGHT: 8"
COLOR: Crystal with Green Snake
STYLE: Glass
COMPANY: Probably European
DATE: 1920s
VALUE: $75.00 – 85.00

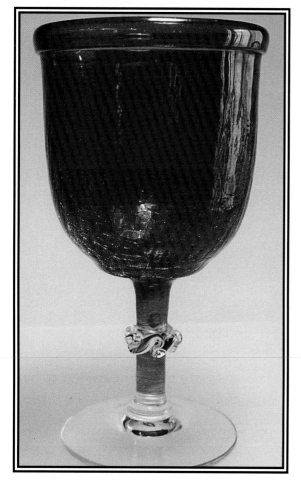

PLATE: 335
HEIGHT: 8½"
COLOR: Cranberry Flash
STYLE: Chalice
COMPANY: Unknown
DATE: Unknown
VALUE: $75.00 – 100.00
REMARKS: From the collection of Dennis & Joan Davis.

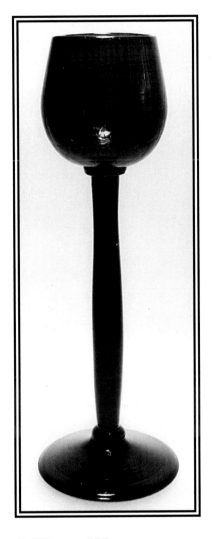

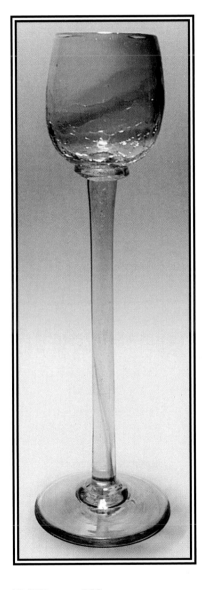

PLATE: 336
HEIGHT: 11½"
COLOR: Amber
STYLE: Giant Goblet
COMPANY: Probably Blenko
DATE: 1960s
VALUE: $100.00 – 125.00
REMARKS: From the collection of
Cheryl & Joel Knolmayer.

PLATE: 337
HEIGHT: 13½"
COLOR: Amethyst
STYLE: Goblet
COMPANY: Probably Blenko
DATE: 1960s
VALUE: $150.00 – 175.00
REMARKS: From the collection of
Dennis & Joan Davis.

PLATE: 338
HEIGHT: 14¾"
COLOR: Amber
STYLE: Goblet
COMPANY: Probably Blenko
DATE: 1960s
VALUE: $125.00 – 150.00
REMARKS: From the collection of
Dennis & Joan Davis.

Hats

PLATE: 339
HEIGHT: 3"
COLOR: Turquoise
STYLE: Hat
COMPANY: Blenko
DATE: 1950s – 1960s
VALUE: $45.00 – 50.00

PLATE: 340
HEIGHT: 4¾"
COLOR: Topaz
STYLE: Hat
COMPANY: Bischoff
DATE: 1950s
VALUE: $50.00 – 75.00
REMARKS: From the collection of Cheryl & Joel Knolmayer

PLATE: 341
HEIGHT: 5¼
COLOR: Amethyst
STYLE: Hat
COMPANY: Bischoff
DATE: 1950s
VALUE: $75.00 – 100.00
REMARKS: Amethyst demands a higher price.

PLATE: 342
HEIGHT: 9½"
COLOR: Crystal with Blue Trim
STYLE: Hat
COMPANY: Blenko
DATE: 1940s – 1950s
VALUE: $100.00 – 150.00

PLATE: 343
HEIGHT: 6½" x 2"
COLOR: Crystal
STYLE: Hat
COMPANY: Blenko
DATE: 1950s
VALUE: $60.00 – 75.00

Perfume Bottles

PLATE: 344
HEIGHT: 2¾"
COLOR: Amethyst
STYLE: Perfume Bottle
COMPANY: Unknown
DATE: Unknown
VALUE: $50.00 – 75.00
REMARKS: Amethyst is a highly collectible color
           and warrants a higher price.

PLATE: 345
HEIGHT: 3"
COLOR: Gold
STYLE: Perfume Bottle
COMPANY: Unknown
DATE: Unknown
VALUE: $50.00 – 75.00

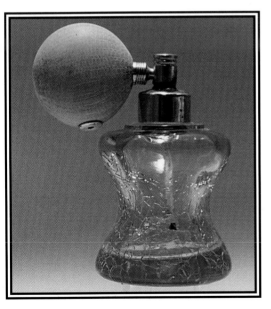

PLATE: 346
HEIGHT: 3"
COLOR: Sea Green
STYLE: Perfume Bottle
COMPANY: Unknown
DATE: Unknown
VALUE: $75.00 – 100.00

PLATE: 347
HEIGHT: 3½"
COLOR: Silver (Mercury Glass)
STYLE: Perfume Bottle
COMPANY: Unknown
DATE: Unknown
VALUE: $150.00 – 200.00
REMARKS: From the collection of Dennis & Joan
           Davis.

PLATE: 348
HEIGHT: 3¼"
COLOR: Silver (Mercury Glass)
STYLE: Perfume Bottle
COMPANY: Unknown
DATE: Unknown
VALUE: $125.00 – 150.00
REMARKS: Courtesy of Bayvillage Gardens & Antiques,
           Amityville, Long Island.

PLATE: 349
HEIGHT: 3¾"
COLOR: Silver
STYLE: Perfume Bottle
COMPANY: Unknown
DATE: Unknown
VALUE: $150.00 – 175.00
REMARKS: Courtesy of Bayvillage Gardens &
           Antiques, Amityville, Long Island

PLATE: 350
HEIGHT: 3" & 3¾"
COLOR: Silver/Gold
STYLE: Perfume Bottles
COMPANY: Unknown
DATE: Unknown
VALUE: 3": $100.00 – 125.00; 3¾": $150.00 – 175.00
REMARKS: Courtesy of Bayvillage Gardens & Antiques, Amityville, Long Island.

PLATE: 351
HEIGHT: 3¾"
COLOR: Light Pink
STYLE: Perfume Bottle
COMPANY: Unknown
DATE: Unknown
VALUE: $50.00 – 75.00

PLATE: 352
HEIGHT: 4"
COLOR: Iridescent
STYLE: Perfume Bottle
COMPANY: Unknown
DATE: Unknown
VALUE: $50.00 – 75.00
REMARKS: From the collection of
           Dennis & Joan Davis.

PLATE: 353
HEIGHT: 4¼"
COLOR: Sea Green
STYLE: Perfume Bottle
COMPANY: Unknown
DATE: Unknown
VALUE: $60.00 – 80.00
REMARKS: From the collection of
           Dennis & Joan Davis.

PLATE: 354
HEIGHT: 4½"
COLOR: Pink
STYLE: Perfume Bottle
COMPANY: Probably European
DATE: Unknown
VALUE: $50.00 – 75.00

PLATE: 355
HEIGHT: 5"
COLOR: Amber
STYLE: Perfume Bottle
COMPANY: Venetian
DATE: 1920s
VALUE: $175.00 – 200.00
REMARKS: Very unusual top. From the collection of Dennis & Joan Davis.

PLATE: 356
HEIGHT: 4½"
COLOR: Rose Crystal
STYLE: Perfume Bottle
COMPANY: Unknown
DATE: Unknown
VALUE: $50.00 – 75.00 each

PLATE: 357
HEIGHT: 6½"
COLOR: Crystal
STYLE: Barber Shop
Bottle/Men's Cologne
Bottle
COMPANY: Unknown
DATE: Unknown
VALUE: $50.00 – 75.00

PLATE: 358
HEIGHT: 6½"
COLOR: Crystal
STYLE: Perfume Bottle
COMPANY: Bonita
DATE: 1931 – 1953
VALUE: $80.00 – 100.00

PLATE: 359
HEIGHT: 6¾
COLOR: Pale Blue
STYLE: Perfume Bottle
TOP: Crystal Fan
COMPANY: Unknown
DATE: Unknown
VALUE: $90.00 – 110.00

PLATE: 360
HEIGHT: 6¾"
COLOR: Rose Crystal
STYLE: Perfume Bottle
COMPANY: Unknown
DATE: Unknown
VALUE: $85.00 – 100.00

Fruit

PLATE 361   Fruit remains highly collectible. It is very difficult to find and is desired by many crackle collectors. Blenko is a company who did not offer it in their catalogs, as it was always a special order item. Please refer to the catalog section to see the companies who did include fruit in their production line. Courtesy of Dennis & Joan Davis.

PLATE: 362
HEIGHT: 4"
COLOR: Orange
STYLE: Apple
COMPANY: Hamon
DATE: Late 1940s – 1970s
VALUE: $75.00 – 100.00

PLATE: 363
HEIGHT: 4"
COLOR: Amberina
STYLE: Tomato
COMPANY: Kanawha
DATE: 1957 – 1987
VALUE: $75.00 – 100.00
REMARKS: From the collection of
            Dennis & Joan Davis.

PLATE: 364
HEIGHT: 4½"
COLOR: Amberina
STYLE: Apple
COMPANY: Kanawha
DATE: 1957 – 1987
VALUE: $75.00 – 100.00
REMARKS: Blue apple in group photograph is also
            valued at $75.00 – 100.00. Courtesy of
            Dennis & Joan Davis.

PLATE: 365
HEIGHT: 4½"
COLOR: Ruby
STYLE: Pear
COMPANY: Kanawha
DATE: 1957 – 1987
VALUE: $75.00 – 100.00

PLATE 365A. Side view of Plate 365.

PLATE: 366
HEIGHT: 4¼"
COLOR: Ruby with Green Stem
STYLE: Apple
COMPANY: Viking
DATE: 1960s – 1970s
VALUE: $75.00 – 100.00

PLATE: 367
HEIGHT: 5"
COLOR: Rose Crystal
STYLE: Pear
COMPANY: Blenko
DATE: 1950s – 1960s
VALUE: $75.00 – 100.00

PLATE: 368
HEIGHT: 5"
COLOR: Amethyst
STYLE: Pear
COMPANY: Blenko
DATE: 1950 – 1960
VALUE: $85.00 – 100.00

PLATE: 369
HEIGHT: 3½"
COLOR: Gold/with Gold Leafing
STYLE: Apple
COMPANY: Unknown
DATE: Unknown
VALUE: $100.00 – 125.00
REMARKS: Peanut shell crackle.

PLATE: 370
HEIGHT: 6½"
COLOR: Amber
STYLE: Apple
COMPANY: Unknown
DATE: Unknown
VALUE: $85.00 – 100.00
REMARKS: From the collection of Cheryl & Joel Knolmayer.

PLATE: 371
HEIGHT: 5½"
COLOR: Gold
STYLE: Lemon
COMPANY: Unknown
DATE: Unknown
VALUE: $75.00 – 100.00
REMARKS: Peanut shell crackle. From the collection of Dennis & Joan Davis.

PLATE: 372
HEIGHT: 6"
COLOR: Green
STYLE: Lime
COMPANY: Unknown
DATE: Unknown
VALUE: $75.00 – 100.00
REMARKS: Peanut shell crackle. From the collection of Dennis & Joan Davis.

Lamps

PLATE: 373
HEIGHT: 7"
COLOR: Amberina
STYLE: Hurricane Lamp Top
COMPANY: Kanawha
DATE: 1957 – 1987
VALUE: $75.00 – 100.00

PLATE: 374
HEIGHT: 7"
COLOR: Light Pink
STYLE: Hurricane Lamp Top
COMPANY: Kanawha
DATE: 1957 – 1987
VALUE: $75.00 – 100.00

PLATE: 375
HEIGHT: 7"
COLOR: Topaz
STYLE: Hurricane Lamp Top
COMPANY: Kanawha
DATE: 1957 – 1987
VALUE: $75.00 – 100.00

PLATE: 376
HEIGHT: 8¼"
COLOR: Amber
STYLE: Hurricane Lamp
COMPANY: Kanawha
DATE: 1957 – 1987
VALUE: $75.00 – 100.00
REMARKS: Courtesy of Bayvillage Gardens & Antiques, Amityville, Long Island.

PLATE: 377
HEIGHT: 11"
CIR: 30"
COLOR: Blue
STYLE: Lamp
COMPANY: Probably Blenko
DATE: 1950s – 1960s
VALUE: $175.00 – 200.00
REMARKS: Courtesy of Bayvillage Gardens & Antiques, Amityville, Long Island.

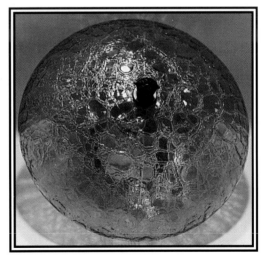

TE: 378
GHT: 12¾"
: 38"
OR: Blue
LE: Lamp
MPANY: Probably Blenko
UE: $175.00 – 200.00
ARKS: Courtesy of Bayvillage Gardens & Antiques, Amityville, Long Island.

PLATE: 379
HEIGHT: 7"
ACROSS: 11"
COLOR: Amber
STYLE: Lamp Top or Bottom
COMPANY: Unknown
DATE: Unknown
VALUE: $150.00 – 200.00
REMARKS: Peanut shell crackle with finial. Courtesy of Muriel Fennimore, Albrightsville, Pennsylvania.

PLATE 379A.
Inset of Plate 379.

Potpourri

PLATE 380A.
Inset of Plate 380.

PLATE: 380
COLOR: Green
STYLE: Watch Fob
COMPANY: Unknown
DATE: Late nineteenth century
VALUE: $75.00 – 124.00
REMARKS: Courtesy of Phil Kleinberg, Long Island, New York.

PLATE: 381
COLOR: Light Blue
STYLE: Jewelry
COMPANY: Unknown
DATE: Unknown
VALUE: $25.00 – 50.00
REMARKS: From the collection of Dennis & Joan Davis.

PLATE: 382
HEIGHT: 4"
COLOR: Blue
STYLE: Turtle
COMPANY: Unknown
DATE: Unknown
VALUE: $150.00 – 200.00
REMARKS: This piece is a combination of regular crackle and peanut shell crackle. Very rare find. From the collection of Dennis & Joan Davis.

PLATE: 383
HEIGHT: 14"
COLOR: Cobalt Blue
STYLE: Fish
COMPANY: Unknown
DATE: Unknown
VALUE: $150.00 – 200.00

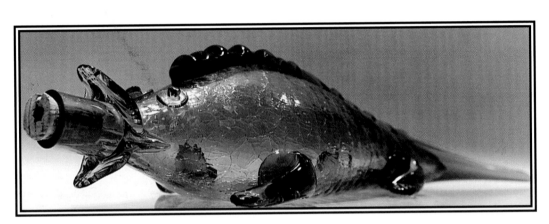

PLATE: 384
HEIGHT: 17"
COLOR: Topaz
STYLE: Crocodile Decanter
COMPANY: Unknown
DATE: 1960s
VALUE: $125.00 – 150.00
REMARKS: Courtesy of Patricia Stone,
           Ridgefield, Connecticut.

PLATE: 385
HEIGHT: 3¾"
COLOR: White Satin Opal
STYLE: Powder Box
COMPANY: Unknown
DATE: Unknown
VALUE: $125.00 – 150.00
REMARKS: From the collection of Dennis & Joan Davis.

PLATE: 386
HEIGHT: 4½"
COLOR: Green
STYLE: Insulator
VALUE: $35.00 – 50.00

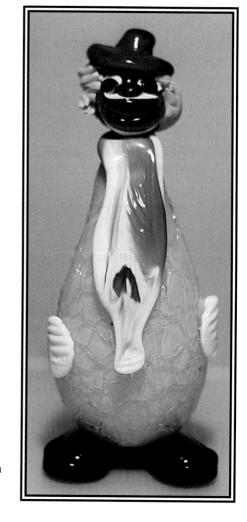

PLATE: 387
HEIGHT: 8½"
COLOR: Multicolor
STYLE: Clown
COMPANY: Possibly Murano
DATE: Unknown
VALUE: $250.00 – 300.00
REMARKS: Rare find. From the collection
           of Dennis & Joan Davis.

PLATE: 388
HEIGHT: 1½"
COLOR: Crystal with Red Bottom
STYLE: Cube
COMPANY: Unknown
DATE: Unknown
VALUE: No Value
REMARKS: Possibly an item that was given at
           or won at a carnival or amusement
           park. If one of our readers have a
           better guess, please let us know.

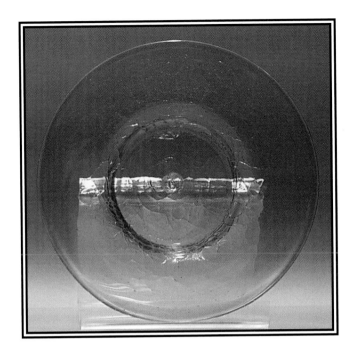

PLATE: 389
HEIGHT: 6¾"
COLOR: Green
STYLE: Plate
COMPANY: Blenko
DATE: 1950s
VALUE: $50.00 – 60.00
REMARKS: Scalloped edges. Vaseline glass.

PLATE: 390
HEIGHT: 6¼"
COLOR: Light Blue
STYLE: Plate (Footed)
COMPANY: Blenko
DATE: 1960s
VALUE: $40.00 – 45.00

PLATE: 391
HEIGHT: 6"
COLOR: Crystal
STYLE: Candlestick Holders
COMPANY: Rainbow
DATE: 1940s – 1960s
VALUE: $125.00 – 150.00 pair
REMARKS: From the collection of Cheryl & Joel Knolmayer.

PLATE: 392
HEIGHT: 6"
COLOR: Blue
STYLE: Candlesticks
COMPANY: Rainbow
DATE: 1940s – 1960s
VALUE: $125.00 – 150.00 pair

PLATE: 393
HEIGHT: 6¾"
COLOR: Olive Green
STYLE: Salt & Pepper Shakers
COMPANY: Kanawha
DATE: 1957 – 1987
VALUE: $75.00 – 100.00

PLATE: 394
HEIGHT: 7"
COLOR: Amberina
STYLE: Salt & Pepper Shakers
COMPANY: Kanawha
DATE: 1957 – 1987
VALUE: $80.00 – 105.00
REMARKS: Labels increase price.

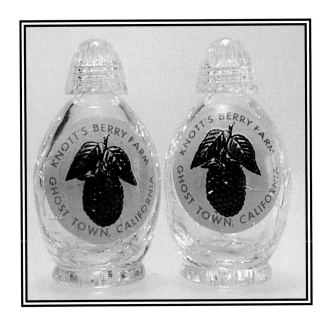

PLATE: 395
HEIGHT: 3"
COLOR: Crystal
STYLE: Salt & Pepper Shakers
COMPANY: Unknown
DATE: Unknown
VALUE: $25.00 – 50.00 (Set)
REMARKS: From the collection of Dennis
          & Joan Davis.

PLATE: 396
HEIGHT: 2¾"
COLOR: Amber
STYLE: Creamer & Sugar
HANDLE: Drop Over
COMPANY: Bonita
DATE: 1931 – 1953
VALUE: $75.00 – 85.00

PLATE: 397
HEIGHT: 2¾"
COLOR: Blue
STYLE: Creamer & Sugar
HANDLE: Drop Over
COMPANY: Bonita
DATE: 1931 – 1953
VALUE: $75.00 – 85.00

PLATE: 398
HEIGHT: 1½" & 2¾"
COLOR: Electric Blue
STYLE: Ashtray & Cigarette Holder
COMPANY: European
DATE: 1930s
VALUE: $200.00 – 225.00

PLATE: 399
HEIGHT: N/A – 2 quarts
COLOR: Topaz
STYLE: Pitcher with Stirrer
COMPANY: Pilgrim
DATE: 1949 – 1969
VALUE: N/A
REMARKS: Courtesy of the Huntington Museum,
Huntington, West Virginia.

PLATE: 400
HEIGHT: 4¾"
COLOR: Crystal with Green Glass Trim
STYLE: Cigarette Holder and Ashtray
COMPANY: Hamon
DATE: 1950s
VALUE: $150.00 – 200.00

PLATE: 401
HEIGHT: 4"
COLOR: Blue/Green
STYLE: Miniature Pitcher
HANDLE: Pulled Back
COMPANY: Unknown
DATE: Probably 1950s – 1960s
VALUE: $45.00 – 50.00
REMARKS: Many companies sold their wares to places catering to tourists. This piece was probably purchased from a Tennessee gift shop.

PLATE 401A.
Inset of Plate 401.

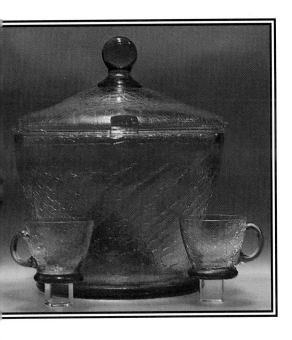

PLATE: 402
HEIGHT: 12½"
CROSS: 11"
COLOR: Green
STYLE: Punch Bowl or Soup Tureen
HANDLE: Cups: Drop Over
COMPANY: Probably European
DATE: 1880s
VALUE: $750.00 plus; Cups: $50.00 – 75.00
REMARKS: Vaseline glass. Very rare find.

PLATE: 403
HEIGHT: Punch Bowl: 10" high, 8½" across
Cups: 2½"
COLOR: Crystal
STYLE: Punch Bowl with Cover
HANDLE: Cups: Drop Over
COMPANY: Germany
DATE: Unknown
VALUE: Punch Bowl with Cover: $300.00 – 350.00; Cups: 40.00 – 50.00
REMARKS: Labels increase prices.

PLATE 403A.
Inset of Plate 403.

Overshot Glass

This form of crackle is called overshot glass, frosted glasswqare, craquelle, ice glass, frosted ware.

It is glassware that was made from about 1870 up to the early turn of the century. Like crackle glass, it originated as a way of hiding defects in the surface of glass. Even though there was an abundance of items produced, such as vases, pitchers, baskets, ladles, dishes, etc., today, it is very hard to come by, not much is seen. The price of overshot glass is very expensive compared to regular crackle glass. Like crackle glass, there were several methods of making overshot.

The first method was to roll a gather of hot glass over a steel plate that was covered with thousands of very small pieces of glass that were sharp enough to cut hands at the slightest touch. The small pieces of glass adhered to the gather of glass. The gather was then returned to the ovens and reheated, melting the small pieces of glass, thus allowing the blower to handle the glass. The melting sufficiently caused the sharp pieces of glass to lose their sharpness. The gather of glass was then blown into a desired shape. This produced a wide thickness between the pieces of glass. The thickness varied from one piece to the other, depending how big the piece was made. The surface of this glass was usually smooth.

The second process involved the glass being blown into the original form first, and then rolled into glass fragments. The surface of these items were sharp to the touch with no avenues between the fragments.

Do not confuse overshot glass or any type of crackle glass with the tree of life pattern. This pattern was always pressed into a mold. Overshot glass was never pressed into a mold, although some were mold blown. If you look very carefully at some of these items, you can see the glass is crackled underneath the small pieces of glass.

Most early pieces of overshot glass were clear. The colored pieces which came into existence a little later on were produced by dipping the gather of clear glass into a pot of colored glass. Some interesting facts on colored overshot glass are American overshot glass was never made with the blending of colors such as amberina; the blending of colors was produced in England; all of the colored overshot glass (not blending of colors) was done by Czechoslovakia (Czechoslovakian pieces are acid etched CZECHOSLOVAKIA).

True overshot glass will fluoresce blue under short-wave light. Some pieces will glow under ultraviolet light.

Some of the companies that produced overshot glass are The Boston and Sandwich Glass Company; Hobbs, Brockunier & Company; Falcon Glass Works, as well as companies in France, England, and Bohemia.

PLATE: 404
HEIGHT: 3"
COLOR: Brown
STYLE: Overshot Master Salt
COMPANY: Unknown
DATE: Late 1880s
VALUE: $75.00 – 100.00

PLATE: 405
HEIGHT: 3¼"
COLOR: Crystal
STYLE: Overshot
COMPANY: Probably European
DATE: Late 1880s
VALUE: $100.00 – 150.00
REMARKS: Sterling silver rim with crimping.

PLATE: 406
HEIGHT: 4"
COLOR: Crystal with Pink Center Flower
STYLE: Overshot Three-section Dish
COMPANY: European
DATE: Late 1880s
VALUE: $250.00 – 300.00

PLATE: 407
HEIGHT: 5¼"
COLOR: Crystal
STYLE: Overshot Jar
HANDLE: White Metal
COMPANY: Unknown
DATE: Late 1880s
VALUE: $150.00 – 175.00

PLATE: 408
HEIGHT: 6"
COLOR: Pink
STYLE: Overshot Ashtray
COMPANY: Unknown
DATE: Early 1900s
VALUE: $250.00 – 300.00

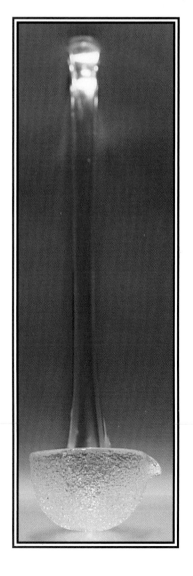

PLATE: 409
HEIGHT: 6" x 8½" across
COLOR: Crystal
STYLE: Overshot Liquor Holder and Dispenser
COMPANY: Unknown
DATE: Late 1880s
VALUE: $300.00 – 400.00
REMARKS: Price reflects if item was complete with six glasses.

PLATE: 410
HEIGHT: 14½"
COLOR: Crystal
STYLE: Ladle
COMPANY: Unknown
DATE: Early 1900s
VALUE: $175.00
REMARKS: Ladle cup is overshot glass.

PLATE: 411
HEIGHT: 7"
COLOR: Crystal
STYLE: Ice Bucket
TOP: Sterling Silver Top and Rim and Handle
COMPANY: English
DATE: 1880s
VALUE: $150.00 – 200.00
REMARKS: Courtesy of Madge Greenblatt, esq., Long
            Island, New York.

PLATE: 412
HEIGHT: 7½"
COLOR: Crystal
STYLE: Overshot Basket
HANDLE: Reeded
COMPANY: Probably European
DATE: Late 1880s
VALUE: $350.00 – 450.00

PLATE: 413
HEIGHT: 7½"
COLOR: Cranberry
STYLE: Vase
COMPANY: European
DATE: Late 1880s
VALUE: $450.00 – 500.00

PLATE 413A.
Inset of Plate 413.

PLATE: 414
HEIGHT: 9"
COLOR: Yellow with Pink and Green Flowers
STYLE: Overshot Basket
HANDLE: Reeded
COMPANY: Czechoslovakia
DATE: Early 1900s
VALUE: $350.00 – 400.00

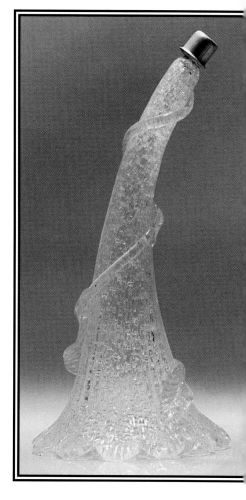

PLATE: 415
HEIGHT: 9½"
COLOR: Crystal with Yellow Applied
             Glass
STYLE: Overshot Epergine Stem
COMPANY: Unknown
DATE: Late 1800s
VALUE: $100.00 – 125.00

PLATE: 416
HEIGHT: 9"
COLOR: Crystal
STYLE: Overshot Pitcher
HANDLE: Drop Over Reeded
COMPANY: Reading
DATE: 1870s
VALUE: $500.00 – 600.00
REMARKS: Courtesy of Patricia Stone,
             Ridgefield, Connecticut.

PLATE: 417
HEIGHT: 11"
COLOR: Pink with Green Glass Swirl and Footings
STYLE: Vase
COMPANY: European
DATE: 1880s
VALUE: $500.00 – 750.00
REMARKS: Green glass swirl and footings are vaseline. Vaseline glass will fluoresce under black light.

PLATE: 418
HEIGHT: 12½"
COLOR: Pink
STYLE: Overshot Platter
COMPANY: Unknown
DATE: Unknown
VALUE: $75.00 – 100.00

PLATE 419A.
Inset of PLATE 419.

PLATE: 419
HEIGHT: 12"
COLOR: Crystal
STYLE: Overshot Liquor Set
COMPANY: Unknown
DATE: Unknown
VALUE: $125.00 – 150.00

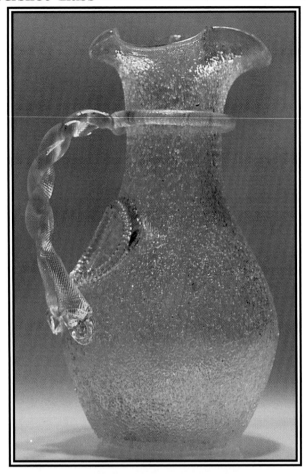

PLATE: 420
HEIGHT: 12½"
COLOR: Crystal
STYLE: Pitcher
HANDLE: Twisted Rope Handle
COMPANY: Boston & Sandwich Glass Company
DATE: 1860s
VALUE: $1,200.00 – 1,400.00
REMARKS: Same or similar piece in Brooklyn Museum.

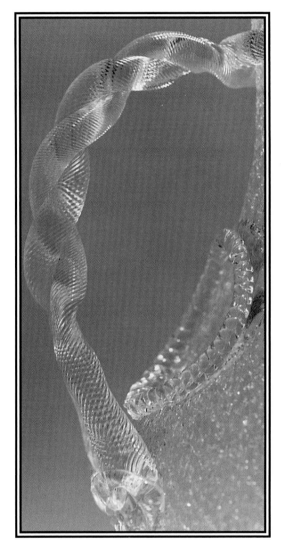

PLATE 420A.
Inset of Plate 420.

PLATE 420B.
Inset of Plate 420.

Old Versus New Crackle Glass

We are constantly asked, "How can you distinguish the old crackle from the new crackle?" Just as with any other collectible, it is very important for a collector to research, as thoroughly as possible, the subject matter. We would suggest that by studying our books, and visiting reputable antique shops, museums, and antique and collectible shows, you will learn to distinguish the old from the new. Much of the new crackle is being imported from China, Taiwan, the Philippines, and Mexico. We can tell you that the styles and colors of this imported crackle are different from the crackle made in the past. The feel of the crackle is also very different, as the new crackle is much lighter. When tapped it does not give off a nice ring, but a dull sound. We believe, that high-quality glass is not being used to make these pieces. Aside from Gillinder Brothers, Gibson Glass Company, Williamsburg Glass Company, and Franek Art Studios, which we mentioned previously, the only other American producer of crackle, that we know of, is the Blenko Glass Company of West Virginia. Blenko has in the past, and continues to be the creator of the highest quality crackle glass.

For years, Blenko continued to crackle specific pieces, such as vases, large bowls, fish, hats, and hurricane tops. They are always developing new designs. Many of the colors used today were not used years ago, as Blenko is always introducing new colors into their lines. This past year, they introduced a western theme. They offered these pieces in beautiful, vibrant, and unique color combinations. Some of these color combinations are azure/emerald, teal/topaz, antique green/cobalt, crystal/emerald, crystal/antique green, topaz/cobalt, topaz/emerald, violet/topaz, and desert green/topaz.

We were fortunate to interview the new designer for the Blenko Glass Company, Matt Carter. Matt Carter has been working for Blenko since 1995. He previously interned with Blenko's last designer, Hank Murta Adams. Matt decides what gets crackled along with designing all the tableware items. He also comes up with the ideas and color combinations. He draws his ideas on paper first, and then working with the mold makers, has the shapes cut out of wood. Although, he stated that he is starting to get back to the bigger pieces that Blenko is known for, about 27" tall, he doesn't know, at this time, if he is going to crackle the larger pieces. He told us that it is very difficult to crackle the bigger pieces. When asked about Blenko's crackling technique, he told us that to get the smaller cracks, you would have to leave the piece in the water longer. If the piece was left in too long, the piece would explode. Blenko pieces are known for their larger cracks. So, obviously, their pieces are not placed in the water for a long duration. (Note: duration of a few seconds.) Crackle glass and other historical glass is on display at the Blenko Museum. You can visit the museum and the Blenko Glass Company, which gives glassblowing tours daily, at their factory location in Milton, West Virginia, or you can call them at (304) 743–9081.

PLATE: 421
HEIGHT: 3"
COLOR: Orange/Red
STYLE: Candle Holder
COMPANY: Made in Taiwan
DATE: 1990s
VALUE: N/A

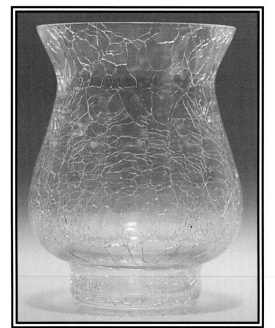

PLATE 423A.
Inset of Plate 423.

PLATE: 422
HEIGHT: 3"
COLOR: Amethyst
STYLE: Candle Holder
COMPANY: Made in Taiwan
DATE: 1990s
VALUE: N/A

PLATE: 423
HEIGHT: 5"
COLOR: Blue/Green
STYLE: Candle Holder
COMPANY: Made in China
DATE: 1990s
VALUE: See inset

PLATE: 424
HEIGHT: 7"
COLOR: Crystal
STYLE: Hurricane Lamp Top
COMPANY: Made in China
DATE: 1990s
VALUE: N/A

PLATE: 425
HEIGHT: 8"
COLOR: Blue
STYLE: Glass
COMPANY: Made in China
DATE: 1990s
VALUE: N/A

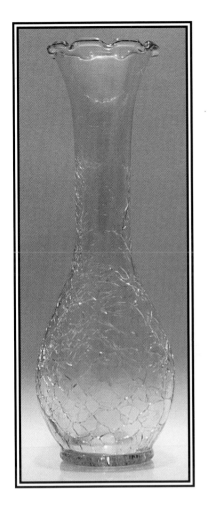

PLATE: 426
HEIGHT: 8"
COLOR: Blue
STYLE: Bud Vase
COMPANY: Made in Taiwan
DATE: 1990s
VALUE: N/A

PLATE: 427
HEIGHT: 8"
COLOR: Blue/Green
STYLE: Bud Vase
COMPANY: Made in Taiwan
DATE: 1990s
VALUE: N/A

PLATE: 428
HEIGHT: 8"
COLOR: Blue
STYLE: Bud Vase
COMPANY: Made in China
DATE: 1990s
VALUE: N/A

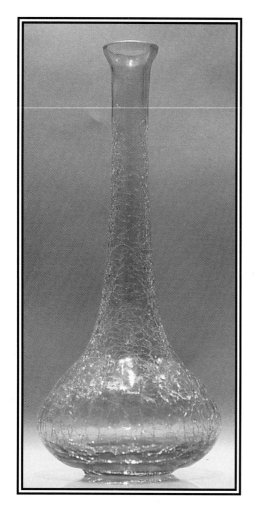

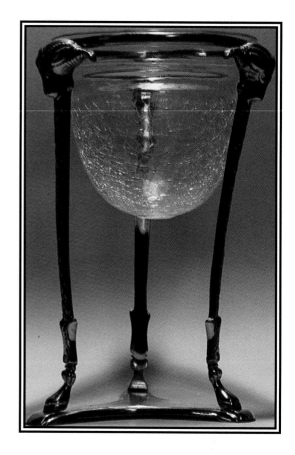

PLATE: 429
HEIGHT: 11½"
COLOR: Blue
STYLE: Bud Vase
COMPANY: Made in China
DATE: 1990s
VALUE: N/A

PLATE: 430
HEIGHT: 10" (Bowl: 5")
COLOR: Crystal with Gold Metal Base
STYLE: Bowl with Base
COMPANY: Made in Taiwan
DATE: 1990s
VALUE: N/A
REMARKS: From the collection of Cheryl &
                  Joel Knolmayer.

PLATE: 431
COLOR: Crystal with Blue Bottom
STYLE: Butter Dish
COMPANY: Made in China
DATE: 1990s
VALUE: N/A

PLATE: 432
HEIGHT: 7½"
COLOR: Amethyst
STYLE: Vase
COMPANY: Blenko
DATE: 1996
VALUE: N/A

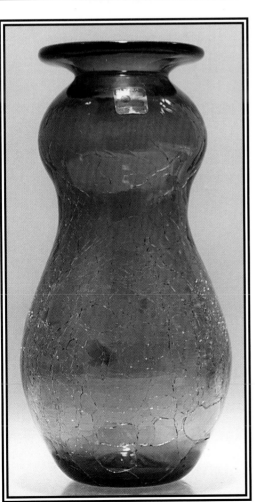

PLATE: 433
HEIGHT: 9⅝"
COLOR: Crystal/Amethyst
STYLE: Vase
COMPANY: Blenko
DATE: 1996
VALUE: N/A

PLATE: 434
HEIGHT: 10"
COLOR: Desert Green
STYLE: Vase
COMPANY: Blenko
DATE: 1996
VALUE: N/A

PLATE: 435
HEIGHT: 8½"
COLOR: Amethyst
STYLE: Vase
COMPANY: Blenko
DATE: 1996
VALUE: N/A

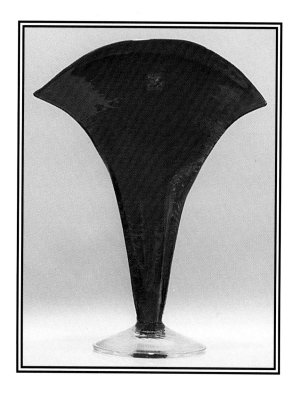

PLATE: 436
HEIGHT: 9½"
COLOR: Amethyst
STYLE: Eggplant
COMPANY: Blenko
DATE: 1996
VALUE: N/A
REMARKS: This is not an item that is crackled in the Blenko line. It was done for us at our request. This was signed and dated by W. H. Blenko.

PLATE: 437
HEIGHT: 11½"
COLOR: Ruby
STYLE: Vase
COMPANY: Blenko
DATE: 1996
VALUE: N/A

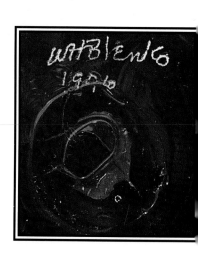

PLATE 437A.
Inset of Plate 437.

PLATE: 438
COLOR: Blue/Green
STYLE: Decanter
COMPANY: Blenko
DATE: 1996
VALUE: N/A
REMARKS: This piece and many other beautiful Blenko hand-blown pieces are sold in the Blenko gift shop.

PLATE: 439
HEIGHT: 14"
COLOR: Amethyst
STYLE: Fish Vase
COMPANY: Blenko
DATE: 1996
VALUE: N/A
REMARKS: This fish is in the 1996 Blenko catalog and is being made in crystal, antique green, and azure. It was made at our request in amethyst.

PLATE: 440
LENGTH: 21¼"
COLOR: Blue
STYLE: Fish Vase
COMPANY: Blenko
DATE: 1996
VALUE: N/A

Labels

When we find pieces with labels intact, we rejoice. The labels not only tell us the company that created the piece, but sometimes give us an indication of when the piece was created, as certain companies changed their labels periodically. Whenever possible, we have indicated the year or about the year each label was in existence.

Pilgrim

PLATE 441. Gold/red/black foil label, 1949 – 1950.

PLATE 442. Silver/red/black foil label, 1949 – 1950.

PLATE 443. Blue/silver oval foil label, 1950 – 1955.

PLATE 444. Black/silver foil label, 1955 – 1962.

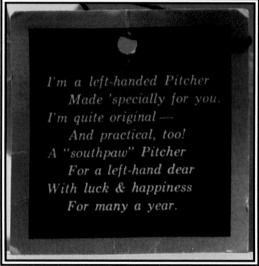

PLATE 445. Black/gold border (front of label), paper label (denoting left-handed pitcher), 1965 – 1972.

I'm a left-handed Pitcher
Made 'specially for you.
I'm quite original —
And practical, too!
A "southpaw" Pitcher
For a left-hand dear
With luck & happiness
For many a year.

American-made Pilgrim Glass
continues a heritage begun in
Jamestown, Virginia in 1607.
Each piece is blown by
mouth and formed by hand,
bringing a touch of beauty
to the everyday business of living.

THE PILGRIM
GLASS CORPORATION
Ceredo, West Va., USA

Blenko

NOTE: Blenko sandblasted the Blenko name on some of their pieces in 1959 – 1960.

PLATE 446. Silver and black foil hand label,
earliest Blenko label, 1930s – early 1980s.

PLATE 447. Foil label with red dot,
1982 – present.

Rainbow

PLATE 448. Silver and black foil label,
1940s – 1950s.

PLATE 449. Silver and black foil label,
1960s – 1970s.

PLATE 450. Silver and red foil label,
1960s – 1970s.

Empire

PLATE 451. Gold and black foil label,
late 1950s – mid 1960s.

Bischoff

PLATE 452. Silver and black foil label,
1942 – 1963.

Kanawha

PLATE 453. Black and gold foil label,
1957 – 1987.

PLATE 454. Round gold metal label (denoting
authentic cranberry glass), 1970s – 1987.

Viking

PLATE 455. Red and gold foil label,
began using this label in the 1940s.

PLATE 456. Red and gold paper label,
date n/a.

Jamestown

PLATE 457. Silver and black,
after 1959 – early to mid-1960s.

PLATE 458. Green on gold,
after 1959 – early to mid-1960s.

Heritage

PLATE 459. Silver/black/orange foil label,
1950s – 1960s.

Toscanny

PLATE 460. Silver and black foil label,
date n/a.

Hamon

PLATE 461. Silver and black foil label shaped like the
State of West Virginia, mid-1950s to early 1960s.
Please note: In the early 1950s a pink and blue scroll-
like foil label was used.

PLATE 462. Silver/black/green foil label, mid-1960s.
Presently, Robert Hamon is still using this logo, but the
colors are different.

Greenwich

PLATE 463. Red/black/gold foil label, date n/a.

Colony

PLATE 464. Silver and black foil label, date n/a.

Skansen

PLATE 465. Black and gold foil label,
date n/a.

We know that all collectors desire to know the origin and value of the pieces in their collection. We hope that our first book *Crackle Glass Identification & Value Guide*, and this book, have helped you all in this endeavor. Unfortunately, we were unable to price the catalog pieces. If you have a catalog piece, not displayed in the value sections of our two books, please find a comparable piece — style, size, color — and you will be able to determine the approximate value.

Pilgrim

Pilgrim styles and colors changed very little from 1949 to 1969 (the years that crackle was a major item in their production line). We do know that amberina was introduced in 1949; smoke gray showed itself for a very brief time in the 1950s; and crystal handles came to be in the early 1960s.

Pictures from 1949 – 1969 catalog.

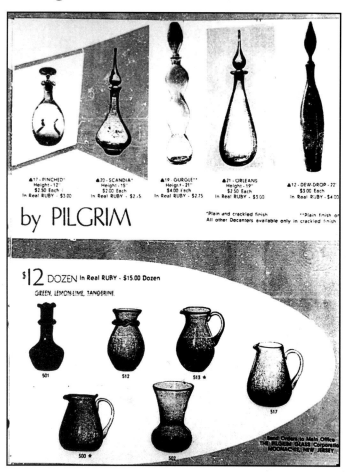

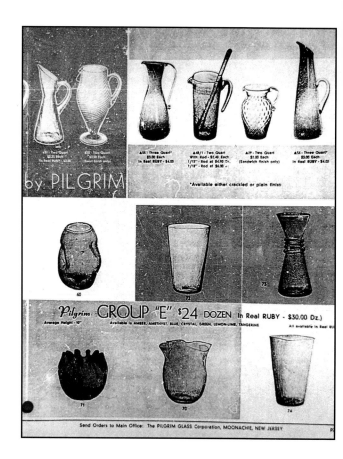

Pictures from 1949 – 1969 catalog.

Arnold Russell of the Pilgrim Glass Company told us Pilgrim continued to crackle into the '70s but in a very limited capacity. They only crackled certain styles, mainly, miniature pitchers. They alternated making crackle "one year on, one year off." Arnold was kind enough to send us his 1970 catalogs for us to photograph.

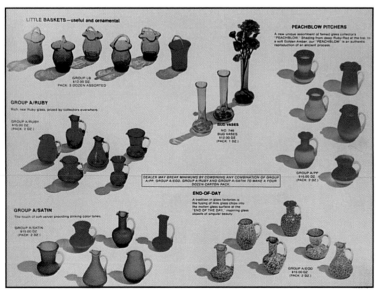

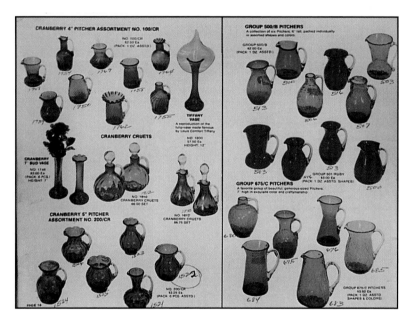

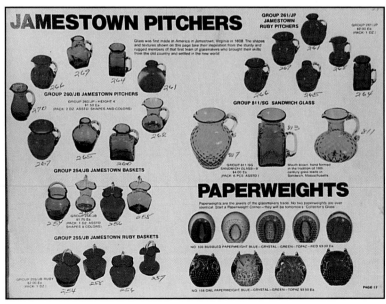

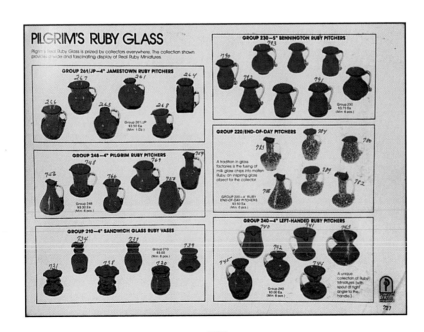

BLENKO

Throughout the years Blenko has changed their styles and their colors. They also crackled different pieces in different years.

Pictures from the 1940s and 1950s Blenko catalogs.

Two of the most popular items we have ever had are the No. 3716 and No. 3744X shapes shown above. The three items at the bottom of the page are all in the heavy Swedish technique.

Colors available: Ruby, Amethyst, Marine Crystal, Turquoise, Sky Blue, and Sea Green

3716	Ruffle Edge Bowl, Depth 6 inches. each	$1.50
390	Crimp Top Vase, Height 7½ inches, each	1.80
3744	Waved Rim Shallow Bowl, Diameter 14 inches, each	3.00
3744X	Ruffle Edge Bowl, Height 4 inches, each	1.00
388	Crimp Top Vase, Height 7½ inches, each	2.50
420	Ripple Edge Shallow Bowl, Diameter 7 inches, each	1.00
453	Melon Vase, Height 7½ inches, each	5.00
462	Square Pinch Shallow Bowl, Diameter 11 inches, each	6.00
461	Tulip Vase, Height 9 inches, each	6.00

New is the quaint pitcher with ice guard, and the unusual handle. The matching glass makes up a different and attractive beverage set. The 3751 set is furnished in crystal with colored rings, and stoppers. The 3749 set is in crystal with colored rings and handle.

Colors available: Ruby, Amethyst, Marine Crystal, Turquoise, Sky Blue, and Sea Green

361P	Pitcher, 80 ounces, each	$2.50
361G	Tumbler, 10 ounces, dozen	7.20
3749G	Double-Ringed Highball, 12 ounces, dozen	12.00
3749P	Pitcher, Height 11 inches, each	4.00
3750L	Pitcher, 40 ounces, each	1.50
442P	Ice Guard Pitcher, Height 7 inches, each	4.00
442G	Mug, Height 4½ inches, dozen	14.40
37	Long-Necked Decanter, 28 ounces, each	2.50
3751D	Ringed Decanter, 40 ounces, each	3.00
3751G	Ringed Cocktail, 2 ounces, dozen	7.20
49	Pinch Bottle Decanter, 42 ounces, each	2.50

MINIATURES

Reading from top left and Bottom left

No. 3516F —Vase. 4½" high. $6.00 a dozen

No. 3516G —Vase. 4½" high. 6.00 a dozen

No. 3516A —Vase. 3½" high. 6.00 a dozen

No. 3516B —Vase. 4" high. 6.00 a dozen

No. 3516C —Vase. 5" high. 6.00 a dozen

No. 3516E —Vase. 3" high. 6.00 a dozen

No. 3516D —Vase. 3" high. 6.00 a dozen

Reading from top left
No. 366L—Vase. 13" high. $2.50 each
No. 366M—Vase. 10" high. 1.80 each
No. 366S—Vase. 8" high. 1.00 each
No. 366X—Vase. 6" high. .70 each

Reading from bottom left
No. 3715L.—Hat. 9" high. $2.50 each
No. 3715M.—Hat. 7" high. 1.80 each
No. 3715S.—Hat. 6" high. 1.00 each
No. 3715X.—Hat. 5" high. .70 each

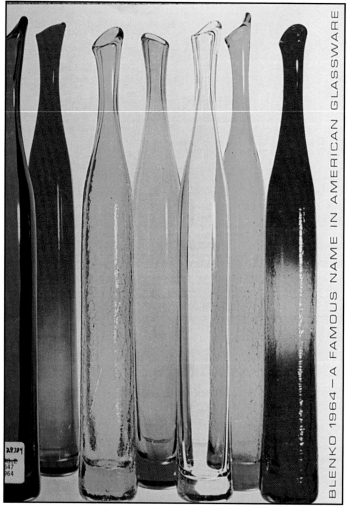

BLENKO 1964 – A FAMOUS NAME IN AMERICAN GLASSWARE

1964 catalog, courtesy of the Huntington Museum, Huntington, West Virginia. Pictures taken by Chris Hatten. Please note: The items with asterisks before the numbers are the pieces that Blenko crackled in 1964. Every few years, Blenko crackled different items, so an item not crackled in 1964, may have been crackled another year. In the 1960s Blenko introduced a system that enables a person with a Blenko catalog, to determine when an item was introduced into the Blenko production line. For example, a piece numbered "6411" was introduced in 1964.

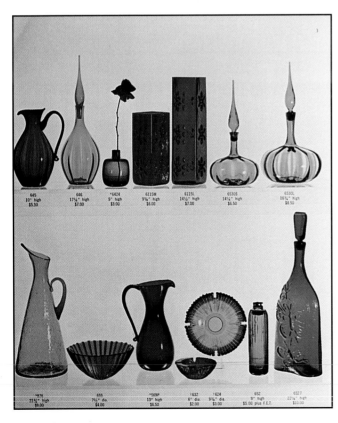

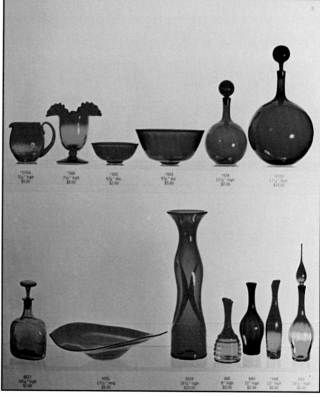

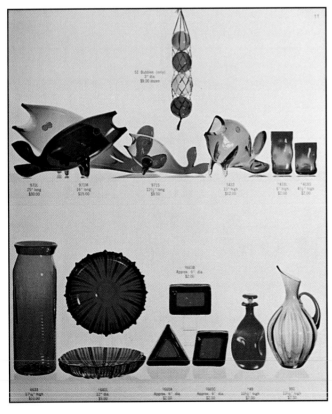

Rainbow

Pictures from fall 1954 Rainbow catalog.
Courtesy of the Corning Museum, Corning, New York.

Pictures from 1966 catalogs. Courtesy of the Huntington Museum, Huntington, West Virginia. Pictures taken by Chris Hatten.

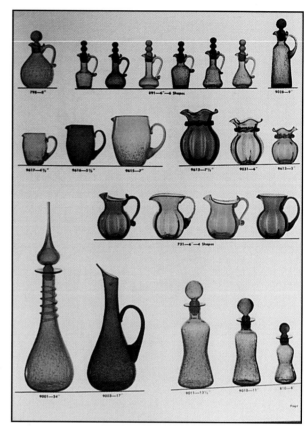

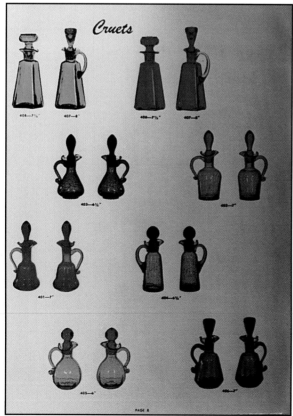

Cruets

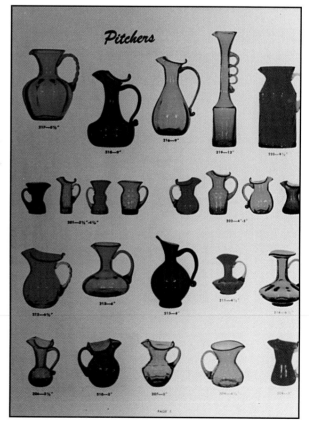

Pitchers

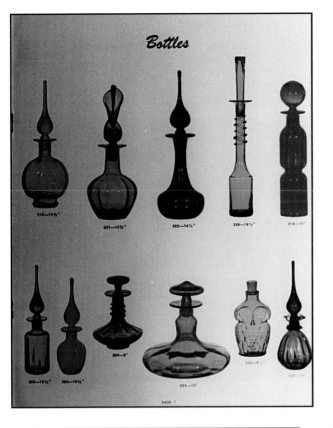

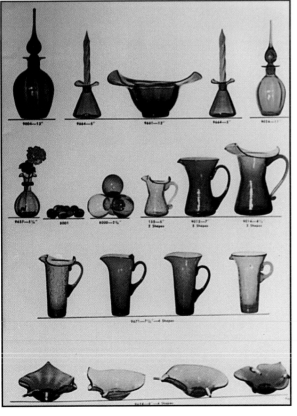

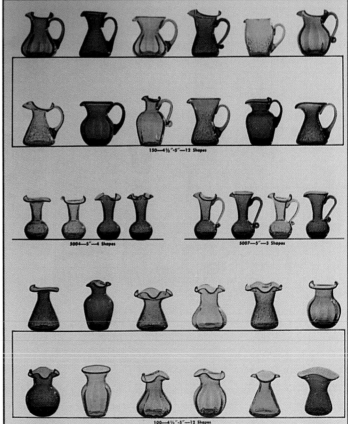

187

Empire

Late 1950s to mid-1960s. Courtesy of the Huntington Museum, Huntington, West Virginia. Pictures taken by Chris Hatten.

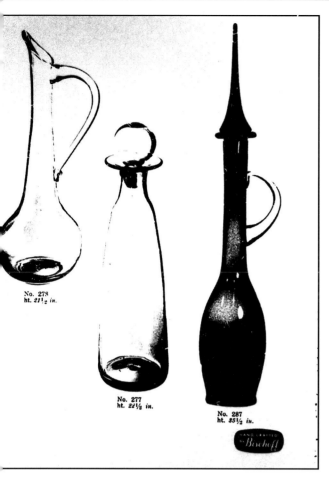

No. 278
ht. *21½ in.*

No. 277
ht. *22½ in.*

No. 287
ht. *35½ in.*

Bischoff

Black and white catalogs, 1950s.
Courtesy of the Corning Museum, Corning, New York.

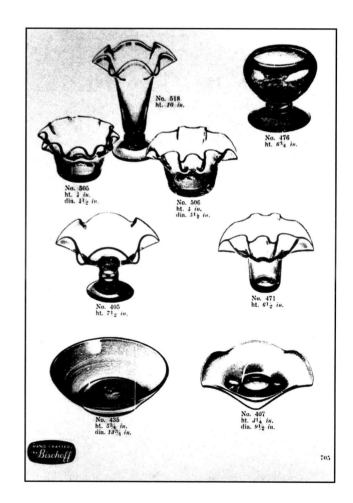

No. 518
ht. *10 in.*

No. 476
ht. *6¾ in.*

No. 505
ht. *4 in.*
dia. *4½ in.*

No. 506
ht. *4 in.*
dia. *5½ in.*

No. 405
ht. *7½ in.*

No. 471
ht. *6½ in.*

No. 435
ht. *5¾ in.*
dia. *13¾ in.*

No. 407
ht. *4¼ in.*
dia. *9½ in.*

705

No. 231
ht. *15¾ in.*

No. 510½
ht. *7 in.*

No. 228
dia. *13 in.*

No. C-510
ht. *11 in.*

No. 269
ht. *10½ in.*

No. 466
ht. *11 in.*

No. 264
dia. *12½ in.*

708

189

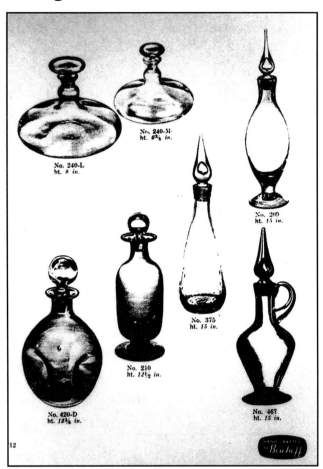

No. 240-L
ht. 8 in.

No. 240-M
ht. 6¾ in.

No. 209
ht. 15 in.

No. 375
ht. 15 in.

No. 210
ht. 12½ in.

No. 420-D
ht. 13¾ in.

No. 467
ht. 15 in.

12

No. C-308
ht. 8 in.

No. 372
ht. 9 in.

No. 600
ht. 6 in.

No. 34
ht. 7¾ in.

No. 550-1
ht. 6 in.

No. 512
ht. 6 in.

No. 421
ht. 6 in.

No. 447
ht. 2½ in.

No. 422
ht. 6 in.

No. 436
ht. 2½ in.
dia. 4½ in.

No. 372½
ht. 9 in.

No. 601
ht. 6 in.

No. D-412
ht. 7½ in.

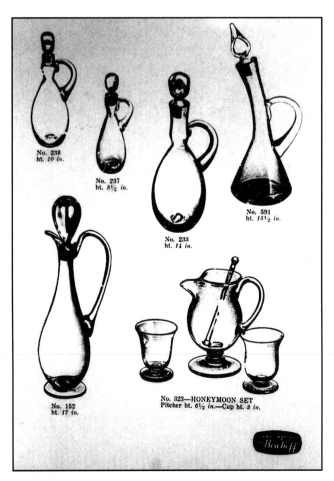

No. 238
ht. 10 in.

No. 237
ht. 8½ in.

No. 591
ht. 14½ in.

No. 233
ht. 14 in.

No. 152
ht. 17 in.

No. 323—HONEYMOON SET
Pitcher ht. 6½ in.—Cup ht. 3 in.

Pictures from the early 1960s catalogs. Courtesy of the Huntington Museum, Huntington, West Virginia. Pictures taken by Chris Hatten.

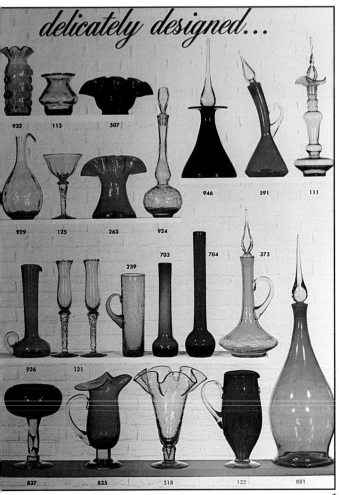

delicately designed...

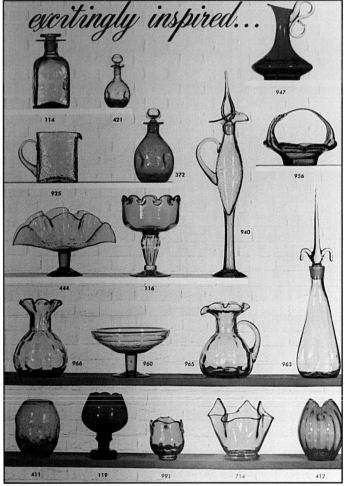

excitingly inspired...

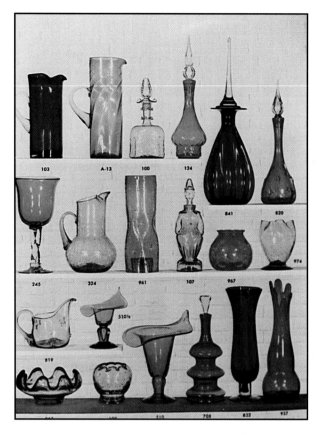

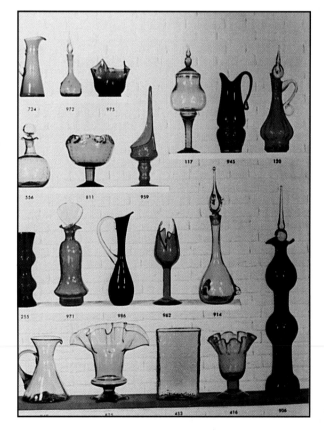

traditionally true...

Kanawha

Pictures from the 1970s catalogs.
Please note that some of the miniatures were made by Robert Hamon of the Hamon Glass Company. In 1966 Hamon Glass merged with Kanawha Glass, each company keeping its own name glassblowing technique.

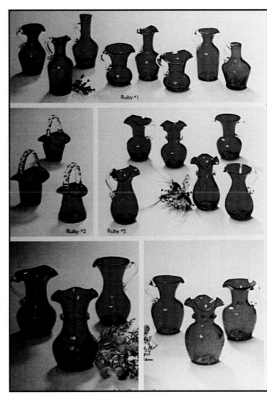

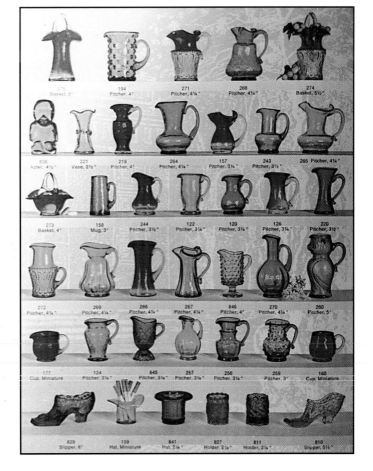

193

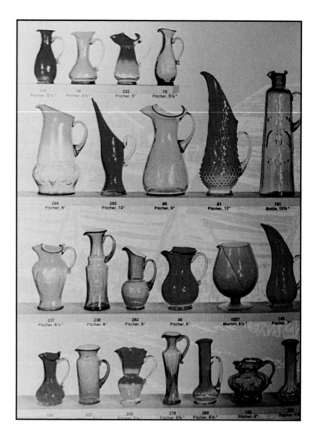

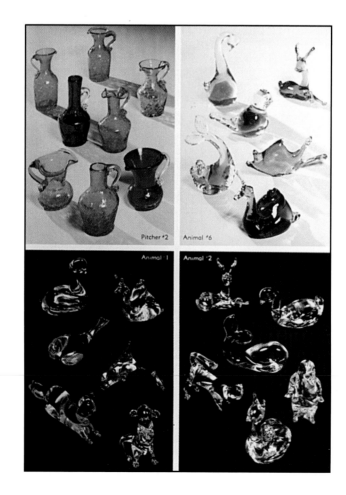

Pitcher #2   Animal #6

Animal #1   Animal #2

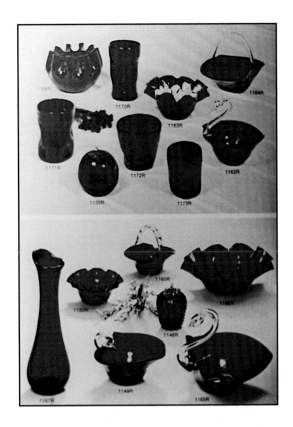

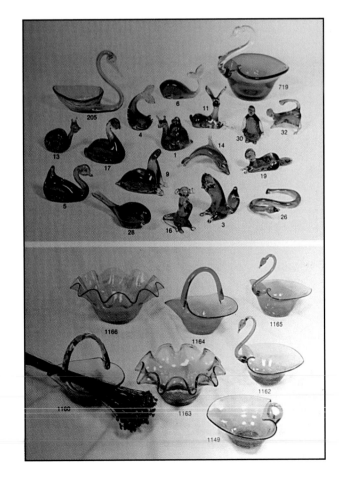

Viking

Pictures from the early 1970s catalogs. Courtesy of the Huntington Museum, Huntington, West Virginia. Pictures taken by Chris Hatten.

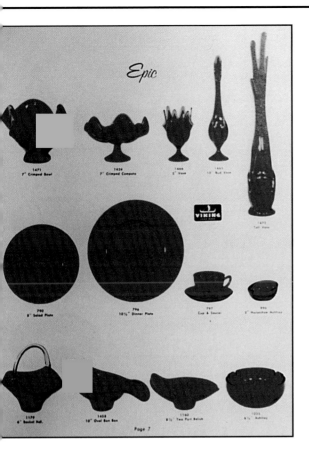

Bonita

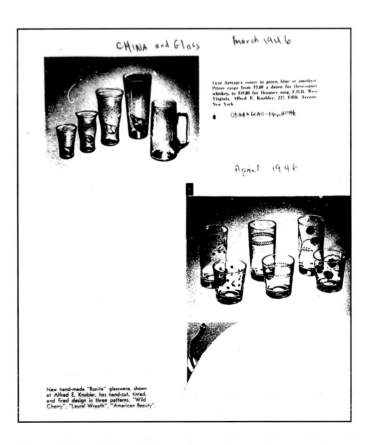

Pictures from the 1945 – 1946 catalog. Courtesy of the Corning Museum, Corning, New York.

Moncer

1950s catalog. Courtesy of the Huntington Museum, Huntington, West Virginia.

Gibson

1980s catalogs. Courtesy of the Corning Museum, Corning, New York.

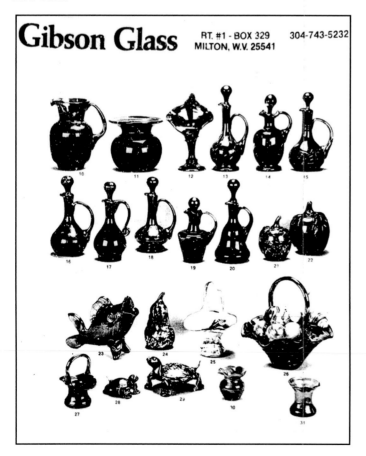

Gillinder Glass

1995 Special Collector's Series Catalog. Courtesy Gillinder Glass Company.

Fenton

Pictures from 1993 catalog.
Courtesy of Fenton Glass Company.

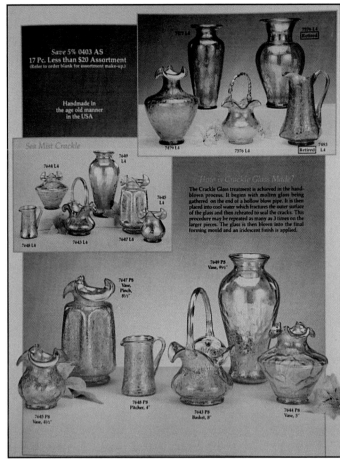

GLASSHOUSE PRODUCTS

ALL of the products illustrated above are hand blown at historic Jamestown, Virginia. The pontil mark is clearly visible on the bottom of each piece. There are, of course, variations between items of the same general class. This is a distinctive mark of a hand made product. All of the items are available in the standard effect which contains a varying degree of air bubbles throughout the glass. This, we believe, most closely resembles the type of glass manufactured in 1608. As indicated on the order blank below, some items are also available in a water-cracked effect, which resembles spider webbing.

Item 2 is copied from mid-seventeenth century bottles unearthed at Jamestown. These bottles may be used as wine decanters. They hold approximately one quart. The standard

seal carries a "J" and two stars in contemporary manner.

Personalized bottles can be ordered with a seal carrying any combination of three initials or stars as shown in the illustration at the left. Item 3 can be personalized also.

Mail orders will be postmarked at Jamestown and can be sent to any point in the United States. Prices include the cost of handling and postage. Because of the limited supply of these hand made products, the Eastern National Park & Monument Association reserves the right to cancel any order and to refund the purchaser's money.

THE JAMESTOWN "GLASSHOUSE," JAMESTOWN, VIRGINIA

Gentlemen: Please mail the following items for which the indicated amount is enclosed.

Item	Standard Effect	Water Cracked	Quantity	Unit Price	Amount
1. Tumbler, 4½"	☐			$ 3.00	$
2. Wine Bottle, 9"	☐			$ 5.50	$
2a. Personalized (specify initials)	☐			$ 7.50	$
3. Decanter, 9"	☐			$ 6.50	$
3a. Personalized (specify initials)	☐			$ 8.00	$
4. Juice Glass, 3½"	☐			$ 1.40	$
5. Bud Vase, 3½"	☐			$ 2.40	$
6. Jug, 5¼"	☐	☐		$ 3.00	$
7. Sugar Bowl, 2¾"	☐			$ 2.40	$
8. Cream Pitcher, 3"	☐			$ 1.90	$
9. Cruet, 5½"	☐			$ 3.00	$
10. Pitcher, 5¼"	☐	☐		$ 3.00	$
11. Pitcher Vase, 5¼" (not pictured)	☐	☐		$ 3.00	$
12. Vase, 5" (not pictured)	☐			$ 2.50	$
			TOTAL AMOUNT HEREWITH	$	

MAIL TO (please print):

Name: _____ Purchaser: _____

Address: _____ Address: _____

Jamestown Glasshouse

Picture form late 1950s Jamestown brochure. Courtesy of Frank Thacker, Williamsburg Glass Company.

Bibliography

Battie, David & Simon Cottle, Editors. *Sotheby's Concise Encyclopedia of Glass*. London, 1991.

Crawford, Thomas. *The Pittsburgh Glass Journal*, Vol. 1, No. 7. 19th Century Glass: Thomas Nelson, 1959.

Edwards, Bill. *Carnival Glass Standard Encyclopedia*, 4th Edition. Paducah, Kentucky: Collector Books, 1994.

Gardner, Paul V. *The Glass of Frederick Carder*. New York City: Crown Publishing Company, 1971.

Husfloen, Kyle, Editor. *American & European Decorative & Art Glass*. Dubuque, Iowa: Antique Trader Publications, 1994.

Huxford, Sharon & Bob, Editors. *Schroeder's Antiques Price Guide*. Fifteenth Edition. Paducah, Kentucky: Collector Books, 1997.

Revi, Albert Christian. *American Art Nouveau Glass*. Nashville, Tennessee: Thomas Nelson, 1968.

Schroy, Ellen Tischbein. *Warman's Glass*. Radnor, Pennsylvania: Wallace–Homestead Book Company, 1992.

Shuman, John A., III. *The Collector's Encyclopedia of American Art Glass*. Paducah, Kentucky: Collector Books, 1994.

Truitt, Robert & Deborah. *Bohemian Glass 1880 – 1940*. Kensington, MD: B & D Glass, 1955.

Wilson, Chas West. *Westmoreland Glass Identification & Price Guide*. Paducah, Kentucky: Collector Books, 1996.

Articles:

Grayson, June. "Crackle Glass," *Glass Collector's Digest*, October/November 1989, Pgs. 50–54.

Catalogs and Brochures:

Bischoff Catalogs from 1950s – 1960s. Courtesy of the Huntington Museum and the Corning Museum.

Blenko Catalogs from 1940 – 1964. Courtesy of Blenko Glass Company and the Huntington Museum.

Bonita Catalog from 1945 – 1946. Courtesy of the Corning Museum.

Empire Catalogs from 1950s – 1960s. Courtesy of the Huntington Museum.

Fenton Catalog from 1993. Courtesy of the Fenton Glass Company.

The Jamestown Glasshouse Brochure, 1959.

Gibson Catalog from 1980s. Courtesy of the Corning Museum.

Gillinder Catalog from 1995. Courtesy of Gillinder Glass Company.

Kanawha Catalogs from 1970s. Courtesy of the Huntington Museum.

Moncer Catalog from 1950s. Courtesy of the Huntington Museum.

Pilgrim Catalogs from 1940 – 1979. Courtesy of Arnold Russell of the Pilgrim Glass Company.

Rainbow Catalogs from 1954 – 1966. Courtesy of the Huntington Museum.

Viking Catalogs from 1970s. Courtesy of the Huntington Museum.